T0065590

Lifting Up Christ

Through the written word

Pastor Fred L. Grant

WESTBOW
PRESS®
A DIVISION OF THOMAS NELSON
& ZONDERVAN

Scripture taken from the NEW AMERICAN STANDARD BIBLE®, Copyright © 1960,1962,1963,1968,1971,1972,1973,1975,1977,19 95 by The Lockman Foundation. Used by permission.

Scriptures marked KJV are taken from the KING JAMES VERSION (KJV): KING JAMES VERSION, public domain.

This book is a work of non-fiction. Unless otherwise noted, the author and the publisher make no explicit guarantees as to the accuracy of the information contained in this book and in some cases, names of people and places have been altered to protect their privacy.

WestBow Press books may be ordered through booksellers or by contacting:

WestBow Press
A Division of Thomas Nelson & Zondervan
1663 Liberty Drive
Bloomington, IN 47403
www.westbowpress.com
1 (866) 928-1240

Because of the dynamic nature of the Internet, any web addresses or links contained in this book may have changed since publication and may no longer be valid. The views expressed in this work are solely those of the author and do not necessarily reflect the views of the publisher, and the publisher hereby disclaims any responsibility for them.

Any people depicted in stock imagery provided by Thinkstock are models, and such images are being used for illustrative purposes only. Certain stock imagery © Thinkstock.

ISBN: 978-1-5127-5335-6 (sc)
ISBN: 978-1-5127-5334-9 (e)

Print information available on the last page.

WestBow Press rev. date: 8/19/2016

"HOW MUCH DO I LOVE YOU?"

How much do I love you? My thoughts will tell.
How much do I love you? My words will tell.
How much do I love you? My actions will tell.
How much do I love you? My character will tell.

How much do You love me? Your thoughts did tell.
How much do You love me? Your words did tell.
How much do You love me? Your actions did tell.
How much do You love me? Your resurrection did tell.

How much do You love me? Your next coming will tell.
How much do You love me? There's no room to tell.
How much do You love me? How much pray tell.
How much do You love me? More than life, death or hell.
Thank-you Lord Jesus, thank-you for loving me

~Fred L. Grant~

THE GENTLENESS OF CHRIST

A~Isaiah 42:3{NASB}~ states, "A bruised reed He will not break, and a dimly burning wick He shall not extinguish; He will faithfully bring forth justice."

Jesus invites all to come to Him and learn of Him

"Come to Me, all who are weary and heavy-laden, and I will give you rest. Take My yoke upon you, and learn from Me, for I am gentle and humble in heart; and you shall find rest for your souls. For My yoke is easy, and My load is light." ~Matthew 11: 28-30{NASB}~.

WE ADORE HIM AS THE EMBODIMENT OF PERFECTION

"For in Him all the fullness of Deity dwells in bodily form." ~Colossians 2:9{NASB}~.

HE IS THE EXPRESS IMAGE OF THE FATHER'S PERSON

"The son is the reflection of the Father's glory, the exact representation of the Father's being, and he sustains all things by his powerful word. When he had cleansed us from our sins, he took his seat at the right hand of the Majesty in heaven." ~Hebrews 1: 3{NASB}~.

"And He is the image of the invisible God, the first-born of all creation." Colossians 1: 15{NASB}~.

Matthew 11: 28-30 gives us an object lesson

Gentleness, which expresses those virtues in man that are acceptable to men, and are a mark of their nobility, and the gentleness of Christ is a revelation of His royal relation to God the Father.

The gentleness of Christ made manifest

1. His rebuke of the disciples, "What manner of spirit are ye" (Luke 9:55{KJV} gives clear indication of the gentleness of Jesus.
2. He always recognized human limitation and dealt with humanity accordingly-Psalms 103: 13-17; John 16:12.
3. He always had a deep concern for men, "Have ye anything to eat?" ~{John 13:33{KJV}}~, "Give them to eat"~{Matthew 14:16{KJV}~.
4. He used the endearing expression, "children" when speaking to his disciples, {John 13: 33}.

Jesus was gentle with everyone

1. Think of His bigheartedness in His invitation, "Come unto me all ye that labor and are heavy laden, and I will give you rest"~ ~Matthew 11: 28{KJV}~.
2. He healed the ear of the servant of the high priest who had come to arrest him-Luke 22:51.
3. Here is food for serious thought on our part. Would we have done that to our enemy?
4. Notice how gentle Jesus was in His conversation with the woman that came to draw water from the well.
5. He knew her life and could have spoken severely to her, but He was gentle-John 4: 9-26.

Think of how gentle He was with Peter on the night he betrayed Him-Mark 14: 72; Luke 22:61.

What a wonderful lesson for God's people on that great virtue "GENTLENESS"

The motive of Jesus for dealing gently with sinful humanity

1. He loved the people, and that is the very essence of true and lasting gentleness.
2. "Behold how he loved him!"--John 11:36{KJV}~.
3. "Now before the feast of the passover, when Jesus knew that his hour was come that he should depart out of this world unto the Father, having loved his own which were in the world, he loved them unto the end."-John 13: 1{KJV}. "A new commandment I give to you, that you love one another, even as I have loved you, that you also love one another."-John 13: 34{NASB}~.

Jesus sees the potential in every person.

And this is why He is the dew for tender plants, Hosea 14: 1-6

1. He died for all because He saw what His redeeming grace could accomplish in their lives.
2. He will have many trophies of His grace, among who you and I will be.
3. It has been said, "Where there is room to hope for anything, there is room to save all things."

Experience shows the following

1. Gentleness is the only sure way of rekindling the spark of hope of lost souls.

    Examples:

    A. The penitent thief on the cross-Luke 23: 42-44.
    B. Mary Magdalene out of whom Jesus cast out seven devils, and was among the first at the tomb of Jesus-Mark 16: 9.

2. The Good Samaritan applied this gentleness to the wounds of the man who had fallen among bandits, Luke 10: 32-36.

Powerful reflections

1. Gentleness in our words is a must for us as Christians--Ephesians 4: 32{NASB}~. "And be kind to one another, tender-hearted,, forgiving each other, just as God in Christ also has forgiven you."
2. "A gentle answer turns away wrath, but a harsh word stirs up anger."--Proverbs 15:1{NASB}~.
3. "Thou hast also given me the shield of Thy salvation, and Thy help makes me great."--2nd Samuel 22: 36{nasb}~.
4. Most of all, our actions must express gentleness.

"To malign no one, to be uncontentious, gentle, showing every consideration for all men." Titus 3: 2(NKJV). See Philippians 4:8, & 2nd Corinthians 10:1 for further study.

"WHAT SHALL I DO WITH JESUS?"

Matthew 27:22-24

First a let's look at the background of this question of Pilate. Jesus Christ, the Son of Man is on trial for His life in the judgement hall of Pilate. His fellow countrymen, the Jews, had foremost in their minds, His execution, though to do this legally, they had to resort to the Roman court system. For the accused to be sentenced to death required the establishment of criminal evidence against the state. At the time of the trial of Jesus Christ, a notable prisoner by the name of Barabbas was also on trial for crimes committed against the state. The contrast between these two prisoners was so obvious that Pilate felt confident that the Jews would ask for the release of Jesus Christ over Barabbas, as it was the custom for the Romans to free one prisoner in an effort to pacify them. Much to the surprise of Pilate, the Jews asked for Barabbas to be released and for Jesus Christ to be crucified.

What was it that prompted their action? Their hatred for Jesus Christ blinded them to reason and justice. They hated Him so much that they violated their own civil code of law, which stated that no one would be condemned to death without due process of their judicial system. They hypocritically appealed to the Roman system that they despised. When we look at this story in closer detail, a deeper reason for their murderous intentions, must be laid upon their moral condition. John 3:19-20 tells us that they loved their darkness more than light. Quoting now John 3:19-20{NASB}, "And this is the judgment that the light is come into the world, and men loved the darkness rather than the light; for their deeds were evil. For everyone who does evil hates the light, and does not come to the light, lest his deeds should be exposed." They did not want the Son of God to rule over them. Luke 19:14{NASB} states, "But his citizens hated him, and sent a delegation after him, saying, 'we do not want this man to reign over us.'"

Actually, in reality, the Jewish leaders saw that Jesus Christ was so infinitely superior mentally, morally, and factually, that they feared that they would lose their standing, and be rejected by the people. It was bitter envy and unrestrained hatred for the Son of God that was at the bottom of this horrendous crime of the Jewish leadership, as Matthew 27:18{NASB} states, "For he knew that because of envy they had delivered Him up." The implications of this action by the Jews is, that they, blindly committed the crime of the ages by crucifying the Son of God. "But put to death the Prince of life, the one whom God raised from the dead, a fact to which we are witnesses." ~Acts 3:15{NASB}~ By engaging in this act, they rejected the choice gift of heaven. ~John 1:11; 3:16{NASB} states, "He came to His own, and those who were His own did not receive Him…For God so loved the world, that He gave His only begotten Son, that whoever believes in Him should not perish, but have eternal life." By sending the Son of God to His death, they, the Jews, destroyed their only hope as a nation. ~Matthew 23:38{NASB} states, "Behold, your house is being left to you desolate!" They committed a most unreasonable act by preferring a criminal to that of the Prince of Peace.

The question of our opening text is as applicable to us today, as it was when Pilate placed it before the Jews. Jesus Christ has placed Himself in every life of every person born into this world. He died for all, as 2nd Corinthians 5:14{NASB} states, "For the love of Christ controls us, having concluded this, that one died for all, therefore all died." This makes each and every one of us morally obligated to have a positive attitude toward Him. There are two basic factors that enter into our decision to accept Him in our lives. 1. Our appreciation of what He has done, and continues to do for us. ~Galatians 2:20-21{NASB}~ states, "I have been crucified with Christ; and it is no longer I who live, but Christ lives in me; and the life which I now live in the flesh I live by faith in the Son of God, who loved me, and delivered Himself up for me. I do not nullify the grace of God;

for if righteousness comes through the Law, then Christ died needlessly." & 2. Our attachment to sin. ~John 3:19{NASB}~ states, "And this is the judgment, that the light is come into the world, and men loved the darkness rather than the light; for their deeds were evil."

Consider, with me, Pilates question from another standpoint. The question 'what to do with Jesus,' will help us resist temptation; because if we yield to temptation, we crucify Him anew. ~Hebrews 6:6{NASB}~ states, "And then have fallen away, it is impossible to renew them again to repentance, since they again crucify to themselves the Son of God, and put Him to open shame." There can be no compromise between Christ and sin; accepting Christ means parting with sin. ~Matthew 6:24{NASB} states, "No one can serve two masters; for either he will hate the one and love the other, or he will hold to one and despise the other. You cannot serve God and mammon." Rejection of God's word is the same as rejecting Christ. ~John 5:39{NASB}~ states, "You search the Scriptures, because you think that in them you have eternal life; and it is these that bear witness of Me."

Prior to making your final decision, consider prayerfully the following. 1. The sin problem—what will you do with your sins without Christ? ~John 9:41{NASB}~ states, "Jesus said to them, 'If you were bind, you would have no sin; but sine you say, 'We see,' your sin remains.'" 2. Consider carefully what you would be losing by rejecting Christ. ~John 5:40{NASB}~ states, "And you are unwilling to come to Me, that you may have life." & 3. Finally, let me warn you that not to choose is choosing just the same; postponing your decision will only endanger your hope. Friends, if you haven't already given your hearts to Christ, won't you do it now? The savior of all mankind is waiting for all who will come, please don't put this monumental decision until a more convenient season as Felix did, which is denoted for us in ~Acts 24:25{NASB}~ quoting now, "And as he was discussing righteousness, self-control and the judgment to come, Felix became frightened and said, 'Go away for the present, and when I find time, I will summon you." There is no evidence Felix ever called anyone to share the gospel with him after this point, and, as a result, died a lost man. Scripture teaches that now is the day of salvation—see 2nd Corinthians 6:2. Friends, please don't put this decision off until it's too late.

BLESSED BE

Webster's New Collegiate Dictionary defines "Beatitude" as "a state of utmost bliss." The Greek word for "Beatitude" is "Makarioi," which means to be characterized by the quality of God. When a person has God living in them, exhibiting His character, they have the kingdom of God within them, as Luke 17: 21 implies. God's reign is already present in the hearts of His followers. The word "Blessed" also means to be fully satisfied, which is a result of the indwelling of Christ in our lives.

The sermon on the mount, which is recorded for us in Matthew 5 and onward, gives ethical instructions for Christians awaiting Jesus' second coming. Today our focus is on the first twelve verses of chapter 5, although we will be addressing other Scriptural passages during our time together today.

Matthew tells us that when Jesus saw the multitudes, the throngs of people, He went up on a mountain. This parallels the story of Moses, who went up on Mount Sinai bringing down the tablets of stone, containing the Ten Commandments, or more accurately the Ten Words. Here, Matthew is portraying Jesus as the new Moses, giving the new law, on a new Mount Sinai. In Jesus' time, the rabbi's sat while teaching or delivering sermons, which is why His disciples waited for Him to be seated, prior to approaching Him. Now the Biblical definition of a disciple is "an adherer who accepts the instruction given to him and makes it the rule of his conduct. This most certainly would include His twelve disciples, though its not clear how many other disciples may have been among the multitudes of people.

Many of the religious leaders, in the time of Jesus, felt as if they had the corner on spiritual matters, as the prayer of the Pharisee, denoted in ~Luke 18: 11{NASB}~ indicates. "The Pharisee stood and was praying thus to himself, 'God, I thank Thee that I am not like other people: swindlers, unjust, adulterers, or even like this tax-gatherer." This was in stark contrast to many in the multitude who felt as if they were the dregs of society, the bottom feeders if you will.

The beatitudes are divided into ten verses, having one beatitude in each verse. In this state, they are similar to the Ten Commandments, as, the first four deal with our relationship to God, and the remaining six, deal with our relationship with each other. Verses 3-11 all start with the word "Blessed", which means having the equivalent of God's kingdom within one's heart. One who is in the world, yet independent of it, one whose satisfaction comes from God, not favorable circumstances.

Blessed are the poor in spirit, these are the individuals who, in their abjectness, need lifting. These are those who, in their minds, know that there is no hope of them ever saving themselves, or of them being able to do any righteous deeds. These are the ones who lean upon the everlasting arms of Jesus, trusting in the sacrifice He made for them, for their salvation. The spirit is the vertical window of mankind, giving them the ability to think about God, which spiritually puts the kingdom of God within their hearts.

Blessed are those who mourn. When people see and understand their sinfulness, they sincerely sorrow in their hearts for their sins. They see that sins, like theirs, is what caused Christ to come down to this earth, to be scourged and crucified. They see that while their lives have been filled with ingratitude and rebellion toward God, God has loved them with unspeakable tenderness. This type of mourning and guilt is used by God, drawing them closer, and setting them free from the condemnation of sin. This contrition brings them to the foot of the cross, where they can leave their cares and woes at the feet of Jesus; thusly they are comforted by the everlasting love of Christ.

Those who, in sympathy, weep with Jesus over the sins of the world will be blessed as well. This combined mourning allows no thought for oneself. While Jesus was on this earth, his heart anguished in such a way, that no language can describe it, about the transgressions of men. His toil, with the all-consuming love to remove the trials and tribulations of humanity. His heart ached for those who refused to come to Him that they might have life. All who are followers of Christ share in this experience, as they grow in in Christ, they become coworkers with Him for the salvation of humanity. They become one with Him in purpose, feeling the pain for those who refuse to come to Him, while also feeling the joy for those who do come to Him.

Blessed are the meek, the gentle. Those who exhibit patience and gentleness under trying circumstances. Jesus puts meekness among the first character requirements for entering heaven, which He demonstrated in His own life. He had no trace of bigotry or severity of mannerisms. He took self out of the equation. He had nature greater than the angelic nature, though combined with His divinity were meekness and humility which attracted all mankind to Him. In -Matthew 11: 29{NASB}- Jesus says, "Take my yoke upon you and learn from Me, for I am gentle and humble in heart, and you shall find rest for your souls". Christians are to be like Jesus, with meekness and humility in their hearts, which makes following the example of Jesus much easier. Those who follow Christ, empty themselves of self, pride and love of supremacy. The soul is surrendered to the Holy Spirit. The Christian's highest place is at the feet of Jesus, listening for His voice to guide them. As the Apostle Paul said in Galatians 2: 20, "I have been crucified with Christ; it is no longer I who live, but Christ lives in me; and the life which I now live in the flesh I live by faith in the Son of God, who loved me and delivered Himself up for me." These are the ones who will inherit the earth made new. The earth that will be recreated back to its original state, prior to sin and the fall.

Blessed are those who hunger and thirst after righteousness, for they will be filled. Those whose crave, strongly desire to be in the state commanded by God, and stand the test of His judgment. Revelation 3: 20 says, "Behold, I stand at the door and knock. If anyone hears My voice and opens the door, I will come in to him, and will dine with him, and he with Me." God will never force His way into our hearts and lives, it is up to us to open the door, and invite Him in. ~John 6: 35{NASB}~ says "And Jesus said to them, I am the bread of life; he who comes to Me shall not hunger, and he who believes in Me shall never thirst." As we mentally come to know the perfect character of Jesus, we develop the burning desire to become completely transformed and renewed into His image.

Blessed are the merciful, for they shall obtain mercy. This is benevolent mercy that involves both thought and action. Not merely by expressing acts of mercy, but having this attribute as a result of the indwelling of God within them, being blessed because of Christ. By nature, the human heart is cold and dark. This is a result of the fall of Adam and Eve in the Garden of Eden, where mankind took on the sinful nature of their new ruler, Satan. Whenever someone exhibit's the spirit of mercy and forgiveness, it is not of themselves, but the influence of the Holy Spirit moving upon their heart. Exodus 34: 6 says tells us that the LORD is merciful and gracious. He doesn't care if we're worthy of His love, He just pours the riches of His love upon us, seeking to redeem any who would come to Him. He doesn't seek to destroy or condemn anyone, but yearns to take away the guilt and shame afflicting humanity. Christ, living in our souls, our very core, is a well spring of living water that will never run dry. Where He dwells, there will be an overflow of beneficence.

Blessed are the pure in heart, for they shall see God. Those who are clean spiritually from the pollution and guilt of sin. The thoughts, reasoning, will, judgment, designs, affections, love, etcetera. These are the things that can actually affect a person's physical heart. Unless a person accepts into their own lives the principle of self-sacrificing love, which is God's character, they cannot know God the Father, the Son or the Holy Spirit. Those whose hearts have been purified through the Holy Spirit living in them, can know God. The pure in heart see God in a new light, that as their redeemer and they long to reflect the image of His character in all that they do.

Blessed are the peacemakers, for they shall be called the children of God. The peace makers are the ones who make peace in others, by having first received the peace of God in their own heart. This is not simply one who makes peace between two or more other people. The sons or a child of God is used as a metaphor for prominent moral characteristics. Those who show maturity, in other words growing in Christ, acting as if they are in fact sons or children of God. They show evidence of the dignity of their relationship and likeness to the character of God. The followers of Christ are sent to a chaotic world, with a message of peace. And by living quiet lives, under the influence of the Holy Spirit, they reveal the love of Christ, by their words and deeds. By this example, others are lead to renounce sin, and yield their hearts to God. These are the peacemakers.

Blessed are they which are persecuted for righteousness sake: for theirs is the kingdom of heaven. Jesus does not offer His followers a life of earthly glory or riches. He does not offer them a life free of trials and tribulations. He does, however, offer them the privilege of walking with Him in the path of self-denial and reproach. When they are able to present the love of Christ, along with the beauty of His holiness, they partner with Christ in drawing souls away from the kingdom of Satan. This arouses Satan to fight against it, and persecution and reproach follow. The character of these persecutions change with the times, though the principle, the spirit that underlies it, is the same since the beginning of time when Abel was murdered. By being a partaker of the suffering of Christ, the Christian is destined to be a partaker of His Glory.

Blessed are you when they revile you. No one was slandered more than Jesus Christ. The powers that be, hated Him without cause. Yet He calmly stood in the presence of His enemies, thusly demonstrating to His followers how to meet these falsehoods, the accusations that were, are and will be leveled against God's people. Christians will suffer persecutions. Just remember this important point--slander may blacken the reputation, but cannot stain the character. As long as we do not consent to the temptations to sin, no power whether human or satanic can bring stain upon the soul. In verse 11, the word "evil" is "poneros" in Greek, which means Satan.

Verse 12 tells us to rejoice and be glad. In the original language this implied the picture of a lamb skipping and jumping for joy. To be glad, then, can be a physical outward expression. The reward we will receive in heaven, (which is the dwelling place of God) is for what we have done and gone through in this life. These are the qualities of the character of true Christians.

THE CROSS AND ITS MEANING

IT WAS AN INSTRUMENT OF EXTREME CRUELTY, 1. It was used by some nations to exact the severest penalty on criminals. 2. Death on the cross or pole was looked upon as a measure against crime, so severe that the very thought of it would send terror into the heart of the lawless. The Jewish nation adopted this punishment, and used it on numerous occasions. 1. The cross is mentioned in ~Deuteronomy 21: 23{NASB}~ states, "His corpse shall not hang all night on the tree, but you shall surely bury him the same day, (for he who is hanged is accursed of God), so that you do not defile your land which the Lord your God is gives you as an inheritance." In Biblical times, hanging someone's body in a tree was considered as shaming the person, (compare ~Joshua 8: 29{NASB}~ which states, "And he hanged the king of Ai on a tree until evening; and at sunset Joshua gave command and they took his body down from the tree, and threw it at the entrance of the city gate, and raised over it a great heap of stones that stands to this day." With ~Joshua 10: 26{NASB}~ which states, "So afterward Joshua struck them and put them to death, and he hanged them of five trees; and they hung on the trees until evening"). Jesus was hung on a tree to show that He bore the curse of sin for humanity. The Apostle Paul was referring to Deuteronomy 21: 23 when he wrote these words, "Christ redeemed us from the curse of the Law, having become a curse for us--for it is written, Cursed is everyone who hangs on a tree." ~Galatians 3:13{NASB}~.

The death of Jesus on the cross on Calvary, changed the meaning of the cross THE SYMBOLIC MEANING: "Jesus Himself established the primary figurative interpretation of the cross as a call to complete surrender to God. He used it five times as a symbol of true discipleship in terms of self-denial, taking up one's cross, and following Jesus (Mark 8:34{NASB}, "And He summoned the multitude with His disciples, and said to them, 'If anyone wishes to come after Me, let him deny himself, and take up his cross, and follow Me.", Mark 10:38{NASB}, "But Jesus said to them, 'You do not know what you are asking for. Are you able to drink the cup that I drink, or to be baptized with the baptism with which I am baptized?" Matt. 16:24{NASB}, "Then Jesus said to His disciples, 'If anyone wishes to come after Me, let him deny himself and take up his cross, and follow Me." Luke 9:23{NASB}, "And He was saying to them all, 'If anyone wishes to come after Me, let him deny himself, and take up his cross daily, and follow Me." Luke 14:27{NASB}, "Whoever does not carry his own cross and come after Me cannot be My disciple)." Holman Illustrated Bible Dictionary, page 370. Jesus intended for the cross to be interpreted in two ways: 1. Death to self, which involves the sacrifice of one's individuality for the purpose of following Jesus completely. & 2. A desire to follow Jesus completely, even if it means martyrdom.

It is now an emblem of victory over sin. 1. Paul uses the cross in emphasizing this point. "But may it never be that I should boast, except in the cross of our Lord Jesus Christ, through which the world has been crucified to me, and I to the world." ~Galatians 6: 14{NASB}~. The Old Testament Tabernacle was laid out in the shape of a cross. Notice the meanings. At the top was the Golden Ark, or crown, which corresponds to Christ's head and the declaration above it, "Here is Jesus, King of the Jews." Next is the golden candlestick, which corresponds to the right hand of Jesus. The table of Showbread, corresponding to the left hand of Jesus. The Laver, corresponding to Christ's body, and the Altar, corresponding to Christ's feet.

Paul, when writing to the Corinthians wrote, "For I determined to know nothing among you except Jesus Christ, and Him crucified." ~1ˢᵗ Corinthians 2:2{NASB}~. The cross has become a symbol of the victory over death. 1. Satan knew that when Jesus died on the cross, it would doom him to destruction, who had the power of death. Philippians 2: 6-11{NASB} states, "Who, although He existed in the form of god did not regard equality with God a thing to be grasped, but emptied Himself, taking the form of a bond-servant, and being made in the likeness of men. And being found in appearance as a man, He humbled Himself by becoming obedient to the point of death, even death on a cross. Therefore also God highly exalted Him, and bestowed on Him the name which is above every name, that at the name of Jesus every knee should bow, of those who are in heaven, and on earth, and under the earth, and that every tongue should confess that Jesus Christ is Lord, to the glory of God the Father."

Hebrews 2: 14{NASB} States, "Since then the children share in flesh and blood, He Himself likewise also partook of the same, that through death He might render powerless him who had the power of death, that is, the devil." Hebrews 12: 2{NASB} states, "Fixing our eyes on Jesus, the author and perfecter of faith, who for the joy set before Him endured the cross, despising the shame, and has sat down at the right hand of the throne of God." 1st Corinthians 15: 26{NASB} states, "The last enemy that will be abolished is death." 2. Not only did the death of Jesus on the cross doom Satan, it doomed death itself. 1st Corinthians 15: 55-57{NASB} states, "O death, where is your victory? O death, where is your sting? The sting of death is sin, and the power of sin is the law; but thanks be to God, who gives us the victory through our Lord Jesus Christ." 3. While we think of the victory of Jesus on the cross, we also glory in the cross because it is the symbol of our hope over death and sin.

The cross and its meaning explored: "...It was an emblem of pain, guilt and ignominy, but has been adopted by Christians as the most glorious badge of a servant and follower of Christ, who was crucified on it...the term cross was used by Jesus and others (Matt. xvi. 24)." Smith's Bible Dictionary, page 66. (Ignominy means disgrace/dishonor). Ignominy, 1. Loss of one's reputation; shame; reproach; dishonor; infamy. 2. Disgraceful, shameful, or contemptible quality, behavior, or act. Webster's New Universal Unabridged Dictionary, page 904.

Here we learn of the attitude of God toward Sin. "And about the ninth hour Jesus cried out with a loud voice, Eli, Eli, lema sabachthani? That is, 'My God, my God, why hast Thou forsaken Me?'" ~Matthew 27: 46{NASB}~. "...Then Jesus cried with a loud voice, saying, Eloi, Eloi, lama sabachthani? 'My God, My God, why hast Thou forsaken Me? As the outer gloom settled about the Saviour, many voices exclaimed: The vengeance of heaven is upon Him. The bolts of God's wrath are hurled at Him, because He claimed to be the Son of God. Many who believed on Him heard His despairing cry. Hope left them. If God had forsaken Jesus, in what could His followers trust?" The Desire of Ages, Page 754. His fear prompted Him to plead with His Father, "And He went a little beyond them, and fell on His face and prayed, saying, 'My Father, if it is possible, let this cup pass from Me; yet not as I will, but as Thou wilt." ~Matthew 26: 39{NASB}~.

"The burden is especially heavy as they travel to Gethsemane, a grove of trees on the slope of the Mount of Olives. Jesus predicts Peter's denial and desertion by the others, and then goes aside to pray. Here Jesus expresses his Commitment to do the Father's will, however great the cost." Nelson's Illustrated Bible Handbook, page 491. Here we see divine love in its brightest colors, "Little children, let us not love with word or with tongue, but in deed and truth." ~1st John3:18{NASB},~ "Father forgive them, for they know not what they do." ~Luke 23: 34.(KJV).~ "This day thou shalt be with me in paradise." ~Luke 23: 43(KJV).~ "Who his own self bare our sins in his own body on the tree." ~1st Peter 2: 24~ "...he saith to his mother, Woman, behold thy son." ~John 19: 26b(KJV).~

Here we see the terribleness of sin in its darkest colors, and here are the facts: Orphans, despair, illegitimacy, insane asylums, empty pay envelopes, war, anger, prison, rape, brutality, divorce, suicide, jealousy, disease, drunken parents, frightened and hungry children, aimless life, homosexuality, delinquency, adultery, atheism, heartache and death.

"...Eli, Eli, lama sabachthani? ...Matthew 27:46{NASB}~. The Bitter Cry, "My God, My God, why hast thou forsaken Me." "But one of the soldiers pierced His side with a spear, and immediately blood and water came out." John 19: 34{NASB}~. The heart of Jesus actually broke!! IT IS HERE WHERE GOD WENT INTO JUDGMENT WITH SIN IN THE PERSON OF HIS OWN SON. "He made Him who knew no sin to be sin

on our behalf, that we might become the righteousness of God in Him."
~2nd Corinthians 5: 21(NKJV).~

These facts make the cross of Christ the great fact of redemption; and we must consider all Bible truths in the light of that eternal fact!! May we always keep looking to the cross of Calvary, remembering the sacrifice made for our salvation!

THE ASSURANCE OF SALVATION

Scripture Reading: 1ˢᵗ John 5: 11-13.

One of the most precious promises in Scripture, in my opinion, is the assurance of salvation. Today we're going to examine this security, the assurance, and the foundation of this assurance. There are six points of this assurance we will examine, then we will examine the work of Christ in this assurance, then we will examine two principles for this assurance.

The Assurance of Salvation:

Security:

Our eternal security becomes a spiritual reality when we trust in Jesus Christ. If we have trusted in the personal work of Jesus Christ, our security is a fact. This does not mean once saved, always saved, people can turn their backs on Christ and what He has done for them. What this means is that when a person steadfastly trusts in the work Jesus did here on earth, to save humanity, that their security is sure.

Assurance:

Assurance is the confident awareness of the security. When we realize what we have as a result of the sacrifice of Jesus, the forgiveness of sin etc. Assurance has much to do with our comprehension of the gift of salvation we have through Jesus Christ.

A foundation for the Assurance of Salvation is the Word of God:

Our scripture reading explained this in clear, easy to understand language. Let's read these verses once again. ~1ˢᵗ John 5: 11-13(NASB)~. "And the witness is this, that God has given us eternal life, and this life is His Son. He who has the Son has the life; he who does not have the Son of God does not have the life. These things I have written to you who believe in the name of the Son of God, in order that you may know that you have eternal life." The Bible is crystal clear on this point. The one who believes in the Son of God has eternal life. Jesus lives in the hearts of those who believe in Him, and through His presence, believers have the assurance.

I would like to examine six (6) points, relating to the assurance of salvation, which affects each and every one of us.

1. Eternal Life: Scripture tells us in John 3: 36 that anyone who believes in the Son, has eternal life. This is also brought out in our scripture reading this morning.

2. Forgiveness of sins: Acts 10: 43 tells us that everyone who believes in Him receives forgiveness of sins, as does ~Colossians 2: 13{NASB}~ which states, "For He delivered us from the domain of darkness, and transferred us to the kingdom of His beloved Son."

3. Freedom from condemnation: John 5: 24 tells us that those who have heard God's message and have believed are free from the condemnation of sin, as does ~Romans 8: 1{NASB}~ which states, "There is therefore now no condemnation for those who are in Christ Jesus."

4. Justification: Which is being declared righteous by God: Romans 5: 1 tells us that we have been declared righteous by faith, as does ~Romans 4: 1-6, 25{NASB}~ which states, "What then shall we say that Abraham our forefather according to the flesh has found? For if Abraham was justified by works, he has something to boast about, but not before God. For what does the Scripture say? And Abraham believed God and it was accounted to him for righteousness. Now to him who woks, the wages are not reckoned to him as righteousness. Now to the one who works, his wage is

not reckoned as a favor, but as what is due. But to the one who does not work but believes in Him who justifies the ungodly, his faith be reckoned as righteousness, just as David also speaks of the blessing upon the man to who God reckons righteousness apart from works."

5. Salvation: Ephesians 2: 8-9 tells us we are saved by grace, through faith, and that it is a gift of God.

6. A child of God by faith: John 1: 12 and Romans 8: 14-17 tells us that all who believe in Him become God's children. Quoting ~John 1:12{NASB}~ states, "But as many as received Him, to them He gave the right to become children of God, even to those who believe in His name." and now Romans 8:14-17{NASB}~ states, "For all who are being led by the Spirit of God, these are sons of God. For you have not received a spirit of slavery leading to fear again, but you have received a spirit of adoption as sons by which we cry out, Abba! Father! The spirit Himself bears witness with our spirit that we are children of God, and if children, 'heirs' also, heirs of God and fellow heirs with Christ, if indeed we suffer with Him in order that we may also be glorified with Him. For I consider that the sufferings of this present time are not worthy to be compared with the glory that is to be revealed to us."

The famous theologian John Calvin taught that we must look to Christ as the objective basis for our assurance of salvation. If we look to ourselves it simply produces doubt and detracts from the saving work of Christ. Look at it this way- when we look to ourselves we tend to focus our thoughts inward, when we look to Jesus, we tend to look upward.

THE WORK OF CHRIST:

Two points here:

1. Our salvation has nothing to do with our works. We cannot work our way to heaven. We are not saved by our works; we do our good works because we are saved. Ephesians 2: 8-9{NASB} states, "For by grace you have been saved through faith, and that not of

yourselves; it is the gift of God, not of works, lest anyone should boast." Titus 3: 5-7 tells us we are not saved by works, but by the basis of His mercy, quoting now from ~Titus 3:5-7{NASB}~ which states, "He saved us, not on the basis of deeds which we have done in righteousness, but according to His mercy, by the washing of regeneration and renewing by the Holy Spirit, 6 whom He poured out upon us richly through Jesus Christ our Savior, 7 so that being justified by His grace we would be made heirs [a]according to the hope of eternal life."

2. Salvation is solely by Christ's person and work as a gift of God: 1st John 5: 5-12 tells us that if we accept the testimony of God, then those who believe in the Son of God receive eternal life. Quoting from 1st John 5:5-12{NASB} which states, "Who is the one who overcomes the world, but he who believes that Jesus is the Son of God? This is the One who came by water and blood, Jesus Christ; not with the water only, but with the water and with the blood. It is the Spirit who testifies, because the Spirit is the truth. For there are three that testify: the Spirit and the water and the blood; and the three are in agreement. If we receive the testimony of men, the testimony of God is greater; for the testimony of God is this, that He has testified concerning His Son. The one who believes in the Son of God has the testimony in himself; the one who does not believe God has made Him a liar, because he has not believed in the testimony that God has given concerning His Son. And the testimony is this, that God has given us eternal life, and this life is in His Son. He who has the Son has the life; he who does not have the Son of God does not have the life."

PRINCIPLES FOR ASSURANCE:

1. Our assurance must stand on the promises found in scripture, not on our feelings. The Biblical order is FACTS--FAITH--FEELINGS. Feelings are the responders of the heart and are to respond to the facts of scripture. Feelings are never to be considered a safe guide in determining what we believe, or our belief in the state of our salvation.

2. Our assurance must be derived from faith in the facts of scripture, not from our works. The works occur in our lives as a result of the indwelling of Christ in our lives. We must be careful not to confuse our works with salvation. The heart, above all else, must be changed, and then the works are a direct result of that change.

Question: does the fact that we are confident in our salvation mean that we can be indifferent about our lifestyle? No! God holds us responsible for what we do with our stewardship, and a day is fast approaching when we will be held responsible for what we have done with the life God has given us. 1st Corinthians 3: 12-15{NASB} states, "Now if anyone builds on this foundation with gold, silver, precious stones, wood, hay, straw, each one's work will become clear; for the Day will declare it, because it will be revealed by fire; and the fire will test each one's work, of what sort it is. If anyone's work which he has built on it endures, he will receive a reward. If anyone's work is burned, he will suffer loss; but he himself will be saved, yet so as through fire." Notice the following: First and foremost, the believer is in heaven because of what Jesus did. The believer is held accountable for what he did with the life and gifts given to him by God.

What are you doing with your life? What am I doing with my life? These are profound questions each and every one of us must give an accounting. It is my prayer that none of us will be found wanting on the Day of Judgment.

A still small voice

~1ˢᵗ Kings 19:11-12{NASB}~ states, "So He said, 'Go forth, and stand on the mountain before the Lord.' And behold, the Lord was passing by! And a great and strong wind was rending the mountains and breaking in pieces the rocks before the Lord; but the Lord was not in the wind. And after the wind an earthquake, but the Lord was not in the earthquake. And after the earthquake was a fire; and after the fire a sound of a gentle blowing."

The prophet Elijah was a man of power. ~Luke 1:17{NASB}~ states "And it is he who will go as a forerunner before Him in the spirit and power of Elijah, to turn the hearts of the fathers back to the children, and the disobedient to the attitude of the righteous; so as to make ready a people prepared for the Lord." "The dauntless courage of Elijah in the days of apostasy and crisis...had made the prophet a symbol of thoroughgoing reformation and loyalty to God...prophecies concerning the forerunner of the Messiah were so strikingly fulfilled in John the Baptist that the common people and also their leaders recognized the resemblance of John to Elijah...Jesus affirmed that John came in fulfillment of the prophecies of the coming of Elijah." S.D.A. Bible Commentary, Vol. 5, page 675.

This power revealed itself on many occasions. In his conflict with the priests of baal-1ˢᵗ Kings 18:21-46. Also In his conflict with king Ahab-1ˢᵗ Kings 21:20-22. He was a man of passion, like other men. It was not too difficult for him to take vengeance on his enemies-1ˢᵗ Kings 18:40. He, too, became discouraged and attempted to run away from his difficulties-1ˢᵗ Kings 19:1-15.

Through a still small voice the Spirit speaks to me. God taught this mighty man some very timely lessons about the presence of the lord. He showed him where God is not, in a most practical way and very impressively too-God is not in a windstorm-Winds of Doctrine-Ephesians 4:14- Winds of disposition-Matthew 11:7. He is not in earthquakes-spasmodic terror. Think of the children of thunder-Mark 3:17. He is not in the fire. Eloquence and oratory are not necessarily God's means to carry the message of truth-1st Corinthians 2:1-6.

He showed to him further where God is. "A still small voice"-in it there is great power. Think of the power of the sun! There is great assurance forever-isaiah 30:15; 32:17. In smallness, King Saul's beginning-1st Samuel 15:17, also David and Goliath-1st Samuel 17:45, Gideon's beginning-Judges 6:15, and Saul becomes Paul-Acts 13:9.

A timely lesson for our day, as we live in a power conscious age. There is no parallel in history as Physical science has done the impossible-Daniel 12:4. Power is in evidence everywhere, in the kitchen, in the barn, and in the field. -Luke 21:25-26{NASB}- states, "And there will be signs in sun and moon and stars, and upon the earth dismay among nations, in perplexity at the roaring of the sea and the waves, men fainting from fear and the expectation of the things which are coming upon the world; for the powers of the heavens will be shaken."

Nervousness among people is on the increase. This is due to the constant uncertainty among the people due to the stresses of the society in which we live. Here are some facts about the quiet life of a true Christian. 1. Their knowledge that their cause is right makes them quite assured-Daniel 2:13; 3:14-18. 2. THEIR ABSOLUTE RELIANCE UPON GOD-2ND KINGS 6:17. 3. THEIR AWARENESS OF THE PURPOSE OF THE POWER POSSESSING THEIR LIVES MAKES THEM QUIET. 1ST SAMUEL 17:42-51; 1ST KINGS 18.

NATURE CAN TEACH US SOME VALUABLE LESSONS. THE MOVEMENT OF THE HEAVENLY BODIES IS SO QUIET THAT THERE IS, AS YET, NO MEANS TO MEASURE THEIR

QUIETNESS AND PRECISION. There is no way of determining the power of the sun, yet it is so quiet that we have no perception of its movement. The lesson for us is this, Quietness is God's method of calming the troubled heart. Psalm 23; Matthew 11:28-30; Isaiah 30:15.

Noise is, as a rule, a sign of emptiness, which has been demonstrated on many occasions. Conversely, as Isaiah 32:17{NASB} states, "And the work of righteousness will be peace, and the service of righteousness, quietness and confidence forever." Christians need to have a special secluded prayer spot, following the example of Jesus, enabling them to hear that still small voice!

"A NEW COMMANDMENT"

John 13:34.

Love one another—this is the mark of light, "But if we walk in the light as He Himself is in the light, we have fellowship with one another, and the blood of Jesus His Son cleanses us from all sin." ~1st John 1:7{NASB}~ "The one who says he is in the light and yet hates his brother is in the darkness until now." ~1st John 2:9{NASB}~ It is a sign of spiritual life, "we know that we have passed out of death into life, because we love the brethren. He who does not love abides in death." ~1st John 3:14{NASB}~ "and because lawlessness is increased, most people's love will grow cold." ~Matthew 24:12{NASB}~ Love is the badge of a true disciple, as John 13:35{NASB} states, "By this all men will know that you are my disciples, if you have love for one another."

The opinion of some people regarding the "new commandment" is that love was not required in what is known as the Old Testament. Jesus states in Matthew 5:43{NASB}, "You have heard that it was said, you shall love your neighbor, and hate your enemy." when referring to the Old Testament. But contrary to the opinion of some people, the facts of the Bible are contrary to their statement. ~Leviticus 19:18, 34{NASB}~ states, "You shall not take vengeance, nor bear any grudge against the sons of your people, but you shall love your neighbor as yourself; I am the Lord…the stranger who resides with you shall be to you as the native among you, and you shall love him as yourself; for you were aliens in the land of Egypt: I am the Lord your God." Also Exodus 23:3{NASB} states, "Nor shall you be partial to a poor man in his dispute."

Contrary to the opinion of some, the Ten Commandments are an expression of God's love, and are revealed in the two great principles stated by Christ in Matthew 22:34-40, here quoting from the NASB, "But when the Pharisees heard that He had put the Sadducees to silence, they gathered themselves together. And one of them, a lawyer, asked Him a question, testing Him, 'Teacher, which is the great commandment in the Law?' And He said to him, 'you shall love the Lord your God with all your heart, and with all your soul, and with all your mind. This is the great and foremost commandment. The second is like it, you shall love your neighbor as yourself. On these two commandments depend the whole law and the prophets.'

Love to God and love to man is the very heart of the Ten Commandments. Deuteronomy 6:5, 10, & 12{NASB} states, "And you shall love the Lord your God with all your heart and with all your soul and with all your might...then it shall come about when the Lord your God brings you into the land which He swore to your fathers, Abraham, Isaac and Jacob, to give you, great and splendid cities which you did not build...then watch yourself, lest you forget the Lord who brought you from the land of Egypt, out of the house of slavery." ~Romans 13:10{NASB}~ states, "Love does no wrong to a neighbor; love therefore is the fulfillment of the law."

The implanted love to God and humanity is the motive power which enables us to keep the law of God. "Whoever believes that Jesus is the Christ is born of God; and whoever love the Father loves the child born of Him. By this we know that we love the children of God when we love God and observe His commandments. For this is the love of God, that we keep His commandments; and His commandments are not burdensome. For whatever is born of God overcomes the world; and this is the victory that has overcome the world—our faith. And who is the one who overcomes the world, but he who believes that Jesus is the Son of God?" ~John 14:15{NASB}~ states, "If you love Me, you will keep My commandments." And ~John 15:10{NASB}~ states, "If you keep My commandments, you will abide in My love; just as I have kept My Father's commandments, and abide in His love."

Why the new commandment, "love one another as I have loved you?" Christ demonstrated true love in His earthly life, as ~John 13:1{NASB}~ tells us, "Now before the Passover, Jesus knowing that His hour had come that He should depart out of this world to the Father, having loved His own who were in the world, He loved them to the end." Christ showed the beauty of loving one another, "and so the Jews were saying, 'behold how He loved him!'" ~John 11:36{NASB}~ What Christ wants us to know about love is that it is a living principle which reveals itself in the life of the partakers of the divine nature. That when it possesses us, it will motivate and control our thoughts, words, and actions, in the same manner as it did the life of the Son of Man. This is the great secret of a true Bible Christian. ~1st John 4:12{NASB}~ tells us that "no one has beheld God at any time; if we love one another, God abides in us, and His love is perfected in us."

How Christ loves us: "In this is love, not that we loved God, but that He loved us and sent His Son to be the propitiation for our sins. Beloved, if God so loves us, we also ought to love one another." ~1st John 4:10-11{NASB}~ states, "For if while we were enemies, we were reconciled to God through the death of His Son, much more, having been reconciled, we shall be saved by His life." ~Romans 5:10{NASB}~ "He loved just the same; that means that while we were God's enemies, Christ died for us. This is why Christ says, "but I say to you, love your enemies, and pray for those who persecute you." ~Matthew 5:44{NASB}~ "Christ loved us to the end, which means that He loves in spite of all the encounters of un-loveableness in our characters. "Now before the Feast of the Passover, Jesus knowing that His hour had come that He should depart out of this world to the Father, having loved His own who were in the world, He loved them to the end." ~John 13:1{NASB}~

We, as Christians, must take this commandment to heart, as the world believes the theory of an 'eye for an eye, tooth for a tooth.' But those possessed by the Spirit of Jesus Christ, who loved first, who loved to the very end, will love as He loved. It must be repeated that what is contained in the new commandment of Christ is the personal application of the love of God in our daily lives, and is then a demonstration that we are truly partakers of the divine nature of Christ, by putting this principle of biblical Christianity into practice. ~James 1:22{NASB} states, "But prove yourselves doers of the word, and not merely hearers who delude themselves."

Also ~1st John 2:4-7{NASB}~ states, "The one who says, 'I have come to know Him,' and does not keep His commandments, is a liar, and the truth is not in him; but whoever keeps His word, in him the love of God has truly been perfected. By this we know that we are in Him; the one who says he abides in Him ought himself to walk in the same manner as He walked. Beloved, I am not writing a new commandment to you, but an old commandment which you have had from the beginning; the old commandment is the word which you have heard." This is a sign that we have passed from death unto life. "We know that we have passed out of death into life, because we love the brethren. He who does not love abides in death."

The divine principle of love has always been the same—throughout all ages. ~1st John 4:8{NASB}~ states, "The one who does not love does not know God, for God is love." Any Christian who claims to know God, yet does not love their fellow man, is living a lie. It is impossible to come to a true knowledge of God without beginning to love our brethren. The decisive proof that someone lacks a knowledge of God is contained in the phrase, "God is Love." Any who do not love, prove that they are not personally acquainted with God's nature. Nominal Christians all too often see God as an angry tyrant who needs to be placated by prayers and penances or the pleadings of His Son. Also please note that God never changes, as ~James 1:17{NASB}~ states, "Every good thing bestowed and every perfect gift is from above, coming down from the Father of lights, with whom there is no variation, or shifting shadow."

In this world, there are many variances of light and intensity, but with God there is neither variance in mood or purpose. God is forever immutable, forever anxious to save lost humanity throughout the world, by every means possible. Not only is there not any variableness in God, there is not even a minute plausible excuse for men to charge Him with fickleness. It was when Christ, the Son of God came into this sinful world, which is full of hatred that He demonstrated with His own life God's love—seen and experienced by the disciples, when Christ said, "Love as I have loved you, for I have given you and example that you should do as I have done to you." -John 13:15.-

THE ORDINANCE OF FEET WASHING

JOHN 13:1-17

It is included in the Gospel Commission of which the command of Jesus is, "Teaching them to observe all that I commanded you"—~Matthew 28:20{NASB}~ It is equally as important to teach men to celebrate the things Jesus Christ commanded as it is to baptize. In fact, faith in Christ calls for constant growth in "the knowledge of our Lord and Saviour Jesus Christ" (2 Peter 3:18)…

Nothing is to be omitted. It is not for humanity to declare that some of Christ's teachings are no longer acceptable. ~John 13:14{NASB}~ states, "If I then, the Lord and the Teacher, washed your feet, you also ought to wash one another's feet." The institution of the ordinance of feet washing was one of the last commandments, given by Jesus prior to sealing the New Testament with His blood. It was to be associated with the Lord's Supper—compare John 13:1-26 with Matthew 26:20-28. The ordinance of feet washing was not understood, at first, by the disciples—John 13:6-12. That shows its Spiritual signification. Had it been a continuation of a menial custom of the Jews, "Jesus answered and said to him, 'What I do you do not realize now, but you shall understand hereafter." ~John 13:7{NASB}~.

Place and purpose of feet washing in the gospel ordinances. He, who is called the Wisdom of God, had a reason for making feet washing one of the ordinances of the gospel. 1. It is a memorial of the great sacrifice Christ made when He took the form of a servant (a slave)—Philippians 2:7. Jesus

33

gave up being equal to the Father during the incarnation, but never ceased being God. He assumed the same nature as humanity, with all the trials and tribulations that went along with it. 2. It brought dignity and honor to an act by servants, considered below the dignity of a Master. 3. Without this ordinance, we could not fully understand Christian humility. 4. It is a test of our true attitude toward one another. If there is pride, selfishness in the heart, feet washing has neither meaning nor appeal to the heart.

Other implications in this ordinance. 1. It symbolizes an inner washing or cleansing—Titus 3:5; Ephesians 5:26. The washing of regeneration. 2. Water and blood are connected with the New Covenant—1st John 5:6; John 19:34. Jesus came "by water," that is, by His baptism, and by "blood," that is, by His crucifixion, which were landmarks in His sacrificial ministry, and identified Him as the redeeming Son of God.

The ordinance of feet washing is a reminder to the communicant to prepare to be clean when approaching the table of the Lord—1st Corinthians 10:21. This is a reference to the wine of the communion service (see Matt. 26:27, 28). This cup belongs to the Lord, it has been consecrated to Him, and is the communion of His blood; therefore it brings those partaking of it into fellowship with Him. Nichol, Francis D.: The Seventh-day Adventist Bible Commentary, Volume 6. Review and Herald Publishing Association, 1978; 2002, S. 747. 2. "Then He said, 'Do not come near here; remove your sandals from your feet, for the place on which you are standing is holy ground." -Exodus 3:5{NASB}-. Holy ground. The place where Moses stood was holy, because God was there. 3. The people could not come into God's presence unless they were clean—Exodus 19:10. Holiness is to be considered seriously each time we approach God. The unholy will not be rejected by Him if they come in repentance, accepting the grace of Christ. He accepts the sinner that He may make him holy, and thus qualify him for fellowship with God (Eph. 1:4; 5:25–27; Titus 2:11–14). Nichol, Francis D.: The Seventh-day Adventist Bible Commentary, Volume 1. Review and Herald Publishing Association, 1978; 2002, S. 596.

It is practiced by the followers of Christ; it is a sacred Christian obligation. 1. This is true in spite of the attempt by some professed Christians to brush it aside as just a reminder to be humble. 2. Their plausible explanations can in no way set aside the implication of our opening text—"For I gave you an example, that you also should do as I did to you." ~John 13:15{NASB}~.

Jesus was doing more than giving an example of service. He was instituting an ordinance to be observed by His followers to the end of time, an ordinance designed to bring vividly to mind the lessons of the original service. The ordinance has threefold significance: (1) it symbolizes cleansing from sin. Baptism symbolizes the soul's original cleansing from sin. The cleansing from the defilements that have subsequently accrued are symbolized by the ordinance of foot washing. As in the case of baptism, the ordinance has no significance whatever unless the participant by repentance and thorough conversion has expelled sin from the life. There is no merit in the act of foot washing itself. Only when there has been the appropriate preliminary preparation does the service assume meaning. (2) It symbolizes a renewed consecration to service. The one who participates and stoops to wash the feet of his brethren thereby indicates that he is willing to engage in the service of the Master no matter how humble that service may be. (3) It typifies the spirit of Christian fellowship. The ordinance is thus a suitable preparatory service to participation in the Lord's Supper. For a further discussion of the subject see DA 642–651. Nichol, Francis D.: The Seventh-day Adventist Bible Commentary, Volume 5. Review and Herald Publishing Association, 1978; 2002, S. 1029. 3. It is included in the Gospel Commission of which the command of Jesus is: "Teaching them to observe all things whatsoever I have commanded you." Matthew 28:20.

The acceptance of the gospel of Jesus Christ involves the use of the intelligence…It is equally important to teach men to do the things Christ commanded as to baptize…Without sufficient instruction in the great vital truths of the gospel, there can be no true religious life…Without genuine love for Christ the doctrines and forms of religion lose their meaning and value. All things. Nothing is to be left out. It is not for man to declare that some of Christ's teachings are out of date.

4. It belongs to the doctrine of Christ. 2nd John 9. The expression covers the doctrine personally delivered by Jesus and its continuation in the preaching

of the apostles. John 7:17. A prerequisite to receiving light is that the seeker for truth must be willing to follow in the light that may be revealed. Nichol, Francis D.: The Seventh-day Adventist Bible Commentary, Volume 5. Review and Herald Publishing Association, 1978; 2002, S. 978.

This is a promise of blessing. 1."If you know these things, you are blessed if you do them." ~John 13:17{NASB}~. Knowledge of duty places upon humanity the responsibility of performance. Humanity is not held responsible for the things of which they are ignorant, provided, of course, that their ignorance is not willful (John 9:41; 15:22; Rom. 5:13; James 4:17). Doing is not to be separated from professing (Matthew 7:21; Luke 6:46; 12:47; Romans 2:13; James 1:25).

It is included in the commandments mentioned in Revelation, "Blessed are those who wash their robes, that they may have the right to the tree of life, and may enter by the gates into the city." ~Revelation 22:14{NASB}~. "Our title to heaven is the righteousness of Christ imputed: our fitness for heaven, the righteousness of Christ imparted, represented by the washed robes. The outward evidence of the righteousness of Christ imparted is perfect compliance with the commandments of God." Nichol, Francis D.: The Seventh-day Adventist Bible Commentary, Volume 7. Review and Herald Publishing Association, 1978; 2002, S. 897.

This commandment, like the others, is based upon love. "If you love Me, you will keep My commandments." ~John 14:15{NASB}~. Love is the motive power of obedience. A lack of essential love is never to be used an excuse for disobedience. One of the best human illustrations of obedience that springs from love is that of children to their parents. Obedience is the natural result of love.

Friends, do you see the reason Jesus Christ gave us this seemingly menial ordinance? As we go through this service today, it is my prayer that all receive the blessings promised by Jesus Christ. "In this is love, not that we loved God, but that He loved us and sent His son to be the propitiation for our sins" ~1st John 4:10{NASB}~.

Bruises and wounds

Jeremiah 30:12{NASB} states, "For thus says the LORD, 'Your wound is incurable, and your injury is serious.'" These words are directed primarily to God's ancient covenant people, showing the reason for their going into captivity: But I believe that they have a spiritual message for the people today: "For whatever was written in earlier times was written for our instruction, that through perseverance and the encouragement of the Scriptures we might have hope." Romans 15:4{NASB} "Now these things happened to them as an example, and they were written for our instruction, upon whom the ends of the ages have come." 1st Corinthians 10:11{NASB}

Bruises and wounds: Our opening text shows the sinner's true condition, as God sees it. Everyone living in sin will receive bruises. That is the work of the devil. ~Luke 9:39{NASB}~ states, "And behold, a spirit seizes him, and he suddenly screams, and it throws him into a convulsion with foaming at the mouth, and as it mauls him, it scarcely leaves him." And ~Luke 10:30{NASB}~ states, "Jesus replied and said, 'A certain man was going down from Jerusalem to Jericho; and he fell among robbers, and they stripped him and beat him, and went off leaving him half dead.'"

Satan will leave no soundness in his victims, "From the sole of the foot even to the head there is nothing sound in it, only bruises, welts and raw wounds, not pressed out or bandaged, nor softened with oil." ~Isaiah 1:6{RSV}~. He will leave incurable wounds: "My wounds stink and are corrupt because of my foolishness." Sin affects the entire body as it is a loathsome thing that is impervious to human remedies. It infects every person on planet earth. All of humanity is inwardly sick, as well as the manifestations of this sickness in their outward appearance. Humanity is close to perishing from this loathsome condition. Psalm 38:5{KJV} and "Who has woe? Who has sorrow? Who has contentions? Who has complaining? Who has wounds without cause? Who has redness of eyes?" ~Proverbs 23:29{NASB}~. Examples: 1. Sampson—"And she said, 'The Philistines are upon you, Samson!' And he awoke from his sleep and said, 'I will go out as at other times and shake myself free.' But he did not know that the Lord had departed from him." ~Judges 16:20{NASB}~ 2. Esau—"That there be no immoral or godless person like Esau, who sold his own birthright for a single meal. For you know that even afterwards, when he desired to inherit the blessing, he was rejected, for he found no place for repentance, though he sought for it with tears." ~Hebrews 12:16-17{NASB}~ 3. Judas—"Now when morning had come, all the chief priests and the elders of the people took counsel against Jesus to put Him to death; and they bound Him, and led Him away, and delivered Him up to Pilate the governor. The Judas, who had betrayed Him, saw that He had been condemned, he felt remorse and returned the thirty pieces of silver to the chief priests and elders, saying, 'I have sinned by betraying innocent blood.' But they said, 'what is that to us? See to that yourself!' And he threw the pieces of silver into the sanctuary and departed; and he went away and hanged himself." ~Matthew 27:1-5{NASB}.~

The attitude of the world when they see you bruised and wounded. Who cared for the prodigal when he was down and out? See Luke 15:11-29; who cared when Judas hung himself? See Matthew 27:1-5. The effects of bruises and wounds: 1. you are incapacitated for doing good. 2. You are losing precious opportunities to prepare for the kingdom of God—"Working together with him, then, we entreat you not to accept the grace of God in vain. For he says, 'At the acceptable time I have listened to you, and helped you on the day of salvation.' Behold, now is the acceptable time; behold now is the day of salvation. We put no obstacle in any one's way, so that no fault may be found with our ministry." 2nd Corinthians 6:1-3{RSV} "In which a crowd of invalids lay—blind, lame and paralyzed [waiting for the stirring of the water. For at intervals an angel descended into the pool and stirred the water. Whoever got into the pool first after the agitation of the pool enjoyed healing no matter what ailment he suffered]. One man there had suffered from an infirmity for thirty-eight years.

You miss the blessing of the great feast of Christ, see Luke 14:16-28, who is able to measure the effects of sin in this present world or in the world to come? Nobody needs to despair or be disheartened, there is a promise for the bruised and the wounded "For I will restore health to you, and I will heal you of your wounds, declares the Lord, because they have called you and outcast, saying 'It is Zion, for whom no one cares!'" ~Jeremiah 30:17{NASB}~ "Is there no balm in Gilead? Is there no physician there? Why then has not the health of the daughter of my people been restored?" ~Jeremiah 8:22{NASB}~ "Go up to Gilead, and obtain balm, O virgin daughter of Egypt! In vain you have multiplied remedies; there is no healing for you." ~Jeremiah 46:11{NASB}~.

There is a cure for the disease of sin, it is found in the person of our Great Physician. People are not sick because of the lack of a means to effect a cure, but their refusal to come to the great Physician. It seems as if humanity has become insensible to their needs. Perhaps many of them are simply too proud to accept the remedy, as that would mean they must admit that they cannot cure themselves. Perhaps many have grown to love the disease called sin, and refuse to look at the Healer and gain eternal life.

It is found in the wounds of the Lamb of God, "But He was pierced through for our transgressions, He was crushed for our iniquities; the chastening for our well-being fell upon Him, and by His scourging we are healed." ~Isaiah 53:5{NASB}~ EXAMPLES: The prodigal son was fully restored—see Luke 15:22-32. Mary Magdalene was restored fully—see Mark 16:9. The woman at Samaria was restored—see John 4:1-29. The lord says he will heal all our wounds, "Bless the Lord, O my soul; and all that is within me, bless His holy name. Bless the Lord, O my soul, and forget none of His benefits; who pardons all your iniquities." ~Psalm 103:1-3{NASB}~ "For the enemy has persecuted my soul; he has crushed my life to the ground; he has made me dwell in dark places, like those who have long been dead." ~Psalm 143:3{NASB}~ "And came to him, and bandaged up his wounds, pouring oil and wine on them; and he put

him on his own beast, and brought him to an inn, and took care of him."
~Luke 10:34{NASB}~

To heal the brokenhearted and bind up their wounds was the great mission of the Son of God, when he came into this sin-sick world, Isaiah 61:1{KJV} states, "The Spirit of the Lord God is upon me; because the Lord hath anointed me to preach good tidings unto the meek; he hath sent me to bind up the brokenhearted, to proclaim liberty to the captives, and the opening of the prison to them that are bound." This is what the prophet Isaiah prophesied, ~Luke 4:18{NASB}~ states, "The Spirit of the Lord is upon Me, because He anointed Me to preach the gospel to the poor, He has sent Me to proclaim release to the captives, and recovery of sight to the blind, to set free those who are downtrodden." This prediction was quoted by Christ as finding its fulfillment in Him.

Christ will bear the scars of the wounds he received for all humanity forever and ever, as they will be the marks of his love for sinners, "And one will say to him, 'What are these wounds between your arms?' Then He will say, 'Those with which I was wounded in the house of my friends.'" ~Zechariah 13:6{NASB}~ Through his wonderful love, christ has made provisions for healing our wounds and bruises. Acts 10:38{KJV} states, "How God anointed Jesus of Nazareth with the Holy Ghost and with power: who went about doing good, and healing all that were oppressed of the devil; for God was with him." The mission of mercy occupied the largest part of Christ's ministry. ~Exodus 16:26{NASB}~ states, "Six days you shall gather it; but on the seventh day, the Sabbath, there will be none." Christ is the great physician of humanities body and soul. As the psalmist, king David writes, "Bless the Lord, O my soul; and all that is within me, bless His holy name. Bless the Lord, O my soul, and forget none of His benefits; who pardons all your iniquities." ~Psalm 103:1-3~{NASB}~

Friends, do you have a personal relationship with the great Physician? Has He touched your heart and body with the hand of healing? This need not be physical healing only, but Spiritual, and emotional healing as well. It is amazingly wonderful to know from personal experience that God is willing to heal any and all from wounds caused by sin! Bless the lord! When we worship the Lord, we must use nothing less than all of our faculties in our worship. Christ wants, and deserves, our total praise and adoration. It is critical to keep the following in mind—in the future, we have nothing to fear, only that we forget how Christ has lead us in the past. Let this be our constant comfort and source of our strength as we continue our Spiritual journey with Christ by our side.

Public Worship

Hebrews 10:25(NASB).

"Not forsaking our own assembling together, as is the habit of some, but encouraging one another; and all the more, as you see the day drawing near."

ASSEMBLING TOGETHER

The Greek word Paul uses for assembling together is "Episunagoge" which means "an assembling together at one place...it does not merely denote the worshiping assembly of the church from which some were likely to absent themselves, but the assembling for corporate worship, not as a solitary or occasional act, but of customary conduct." (Key word Bible, Greek lexicon Section, page 1834). This admonition of Paul is timely and in accord with: 1. Ancient practice among God's people—Leviticus 23:1-38; Psalm 89:7; 107:32; 111:1. 2. The Patriarchs built altars wherever they pitched their tents—Genesis 8:20; 12:7; 22:9; 35:1. The entire assembly of Israel came together as one to celebrate the Sabbath and the many feasts prescribed by God. God is respected in the assembly/church. The assembly of the saints represents the divine counsel in heaven. We are to praise God in the assembly, in the congregation. The patriarchs built altars and their entire households worshiped. Public worship is practiced by most all religionists all over the world: Acts 17:23

New Testament examples:

(a). Christ attended public worship. It was His custom to meet with the people in public worship—Luke 4:16. (b). The Disciples of Christ attended public worship—Acts 3:1-9; 16:13; 17:1-9. (c). Not to attend is contrary to the Lord's counsel—Hebrews 10:25-26. The Sabbath is prominent in the ministry of Jesus, and is, in a very special sense, His day. Jesus' disciples worshiped publicly. The disciples worshiped wherever and with whomever were worshiping. The Apostle Paul's custom was to worship in the synagogue on the Sabbath.

A few important reasons for public worship:

(a). On Christ's account. He made a promise, "For where two or three are gathered together in my name, there am I in the midst of them." Matthew 18:20. (b). On the church's account. The church is called "assembly"— James 2:2; Hebrews 12:23. It is in the assembly of the church where spiritual gifts are manifested—1st Corinthians 12:1-28; Ephesians 4:11-12. Christians are to come together even if there are only a small number of individuals. The assembly, is quite literally the Synagogue, and would be called the church building today. It is the privilege of believers to come together, sharing a spirit of oneness with each other, continuing with the example of Jesus, the apostles, and believers who came prior. The assembly/church is where the spiritual gifts are manifest in the lives of believers. Believers come to church to edify each other.

It is in the assembly of the church where communion is served—1st Corinthians 11:23-24. But we ought to attend the church services for our own sakes, which is foremost. We are in need of the blessings waiting for us at the church. Church is where communion is observed, where the Christian eats the bread and drinks the wine, symbolizing unity and mutual partnership with God and fellow believers. Isaiah 66:22-23 tells us that we will come together as an assembly, worshiping God from one Sabbath to another in heaven. Why wouldn't we worship together now, every Sabbath in preparation for heaven?

Specific reasons for attending public worship:

(a). "Exhorting one another"—Hebrews 3:13. To exhort is to encourage each other in the Lord—1st Peter 5:1. (b). Exhortation takes place in public gatherings—1st Corinthians 11:20. (c). This exhortation should be to watchfulness and prayerful vigilance—Matthew 24:42-44; 1st Peter 5:8; to courage and perseverance—Matthew 24:12, 14; Revelation 2:10. Scripture teaches that we are to continuously exhort, edify, build up and encourage each other. Not only are we to edify each other, but also the elders and other leaders in the church. The best way to edify, exhort and encourage others is to be in fellowship with them on a regular basis. Believers must come together for prayer and Bible study. This strengthens, and enables believers to withstand "wolves in sheep's clothing" from introducing false teachings into their midst. This coming together helps keep the fire of Christian love from growing cold, and dying out. Christians must unite, which enables them to fulfill the great gospel commission of spreading the gospel to the entire world. The fulfillment of this gospel commission cannot and quite frankly, will not be completed until God's people, come together, uniting in purpose to finish His work. Those who are faithful to the end will receive the crown of life, when Jesus takes us all to heaven.

A powerful motive:

"As you see the day approaching." While the apostle Paul was writing these words, could he have been thinking about the trials and persecutions that the early Christians were facing? He, himself had persecuted many Christians prior to his conversion. (a). We face similar conditions approaching indicative of the last days—Revelation 12:17; Hebrews 11:36-40; Acts 8:1-4. (b). It seems to me that Paul had S.D.A.'s in mind when he admonishes the believers to meet together and exhort one another because we do know that we are nearing the time of persecution—the fulfillment of Bible Prophecy.

We, as Christians, will soon face a time of trouble that is unparalleled in human history. It will be virtually impossible for us to stand alone in the coming perilous times. We must come together now, building up the believers in preparation for the coming time of trouble. As Christian believers were persecuted during the time of Saul/Paul, and later during the dark ages, so shall it happen once again. This all will happen just prior to the second coming of Jesus Christ. We have four specific fulfillments of Bible prophecy to show that the end is near at hand: Revelation 13:11-17—developments in the U.S.A.; the emergence of the Papacy; and the leaning of nominal Protestantism toward Rome. The moral breakdown of the home, society, and the nations—2nd Timothy 3:1-9; Matthew 24:12. Conditions in our church cannot be ignored—Revelation 3:14-17. One day, the peace and freedom, which we have to worship as we please, will come to an end.

Towards the end of time, people will exhibit traits openly, that so far have been held in check. People will display a form of Godliness, but in their hearts, they will deny its power. They will resist the plain teaching of truth found in Scripture, preferring their own traditions. We, as a church, must wake up! We must heed the clear warnings of Scripture, we cannot stay lukewarm, but we must catch on fire. 4. The signs foretelling the coming of our Lord have all, except the Mark of the Beast, been fulfilled. Surely we have many reasons to heed Paul's admonition to assemble ourselves and to use these gatherings for prayerful exhortation and encouragement, because the end of all things is upon us—Romans 13:11-14.

We must put on Christ!!

We, as Christians, must be conscience of our conduct. What we once did prior to becoming believers, we now choose not to do. The Christian life is characterized by moral purity and transparency. Our conduct must be adopted from the conduct and spirit of Jesus Christ.

Soon and very soon, we will see Jesus coming in the eastern sky, saying "well done good and faithful servant"

I want to go home with Him!! How about you?

LAW AND GRACE

Romans 7:12

Law and grace are two subjects which there is considerable difference of opinion. There are those, who believe and teach, that the law and grace are contrary to one another; that they do not mix. There are others, who believe and teach, that since no sinner can keep the law, God, in His mercy, supplanted the law by placing humanity under grace. Here's a novel concept, why don't we let the Bible solve this issue for us? Let's ask the following questions: 1. What does the Bible teach about law and grace? 2. Are they against each other? & 3. Does grace nullify God's law?

First, the nature and relationship of law and grace. The law of the Ten Commandments are a revelation of God's character and an expression of His eternal and unchangeable will. The Law of the Ten Commandments are found in Exodus 20:1-17 and many other places in Scripture, and they are a revelation of His nature and the nature of His government. Romans 7:12{NASB} states, "So then the Law is holy, and the commandment is holy and righteous and good." Far from the law being sin, see Romans 7:7, it is holy and pure, and as a revelation of the character of its author and all expression of His mind and will, the law of God could be nothing other than true, righteous and holy. Psalm 111:8-9{NASB} when referring to the Law of God states, "They are upheld forever and ever; they are performed in truth and uprightness. He has sent redemption to His people; He has ordained His covenant forever; Holy and awesome is His name." Also Luke 16:17{NASB} states, "But it is easier for heaven and earth to pass away than for one stroke of a letter of the Law to fail."

The Law of the Ten Commandments are an expression of His eternal and unchangeable will by which He regulates the moral relationship between man and God, and man and man. Romans 2:17{NASB} states, "But if you bear the name 'Jew," and rely upon the Law and boast in God." In the book of Romans so far, Paul has shown that Gentiles have sinned. He has explained that Jews and Gentiles alike are subject to God's impartial judgment. In this verse, Paul is showing that Jews along with gentiles are guilty of the same sins, of which some of the Jews were ready to condemn the gentiles. Paul, here, is proving that all humanity is are under the condemnation and in need of the righteousness and salvation of the gospel, see also Luke 10:25; & the story of the rich young ruler in Matthew 19:16-19. The Ten Commandments are summed up in the two commandments found in Matthew 22:36-40, here quoting from the nasb, "Teacher, which is the great commandment in the Law?' And He said to him, 'You shall love the Lord your God with all your soul, and with all your mind, this is the greatest and foremost commandment. The second is like it, you shall love your neighbor as yourself. On these two commandments depend the whole Law and the Prophets.'"

The grace of God is God's unmerited favor toward sinners. Salvation by grace excludes the works of the law. Ephesians 2:7-9{NASB} states, "In order that in the ages to come He might show the surpassing riches of His grace in kindness toward us in Christ Jesus. For by grace you have been saved through faith; and that not of yourselves, it is the gift of God, not as a result of works, that no one should boast." Romans 3:20{NASB} states, "Because by the works of the Law no flesh will be justified in His sight; for through the Law comes the knowledge of sin." And Romans 11:6{NASB} states, "But if it is by grace, it is no longer on the basis of works, otherwise grace is no longer grace."

A broken law cannot save the guilty, it can only condemn them. Romans 3:19{NASB} states, "Now we know that whatever the Law says, it speaks to those who are under the Law, that every mouth may be closed, and all the world may become accountable to God." Also James 1:22-24{NASB} states, "But prove yourselves doers of the word, and not merely hearers who delude themselves. For if anyone is a hearer of the word and not a doer, he is like a man who looks at his natural face in a mirror, for once he has looked at himself and gone away, he has immediately forgotten what kind of person he was." The grace of God is an expression of a loving Father to sinners; a willingness to forgive our sins and to redeem us from the eternal consequences of sin.

The truths about the nature and relationship are too often overlooked by some people. Grace is never a license for breaking God's law! I would ask each to prayerfully read Romans 6:1-12, letting the words of Scripture speak to you, while not inserting your own ideas and opinions into the text. Galatians 2:16-19{NASB} states, "Now the promises were spoken to Abraham and to his seed. He does not say, and to seeds, as referring to many, but rather to one, and to your seed, that is Christ. What I am saying is this: the Law, which came four hundred and thirty years later, does not invalidate a covenant previously ratified by God, so as to nullify the promise. Why the Law then? It was added because of transgressions, having been ordained through angels by the agency of a mediator, until the seed should come to whom the promise had been made."

The following are some vivid examples of the obligations of grace. Jesus talking to the adulterous woman in John 8:11{NASB} which states, "And she said, 'no one, Lord.' And Jesus said, 'Neither do I condemn you; go your way. From now on sin no more.'" Jesus healing the paralytic man by the pool of Bethesda, "Afterward Jesus found him in the temple, and said to him, 'Behold, you have become well; do not sin anymore, so that nothing worse may befall you.'" ~John 5:14{NASB}~

Who is under grace and who is under the law? 1. Everyone who accepts Jesus Christ as their personal savior is under grace. Romans 8:1{NASB} states, "There is therefore now no condemnation for those who are in Christ Jesus." 2. Conversely, everyone who breaks God's law is under the law. Romans 3:19{NASB} states, "Now we know that whatever the Law says, it speaks to those who are under the Law, that every mouth may be closed, and all the world may become accountable to God. The following are two impressive examples. Two men went into the temple to worship, one was a Pharisee and the other was a despised tax collector; both were sinners—one came as a sinner and left as a sinner, the other came as a sinner, but left under the dispensation of grace. Luke 18:10-14{NASB} states, "Two men went up into the temple to pray, one a Pharisee, and the other a tax-gatherer. The Pharisee stood and was praying thus to himself, 'God, I thank Thee that I am not like other people: swindlers, unjust, adulterers, or even like this tax-gatherer. I fast twice a week; I pay tithes of all that I get.' But the tax-gatherer, standing some distance away, was even unwilling to lift up his eyes to heaven, but was beating his breast, saying, 'God, be merciful to me, the sinner!' I tell you, this man went down to his house justified rather than the other; for everyone who exalts himself shall be humbled, but he who humbles himself shall be exalted.'"

Law and grace come from the same source, from God; both serve a purpose in God's plan for humanity. One reveals God's will; the other enables us to do God's will. One convicts of sin; the other pardons our sin. God's moral Law, the Ten Commandments, are in force everywhere, and at all times, for it is a reflection of His very being. It has never been abrogated, nor indeed can be. Grace signifies God's kindness toward humanity. Grace is, without equivocation identified as the medium or instrument through which God has effected the salvation of all believers. Grace is the sustaining influence enabling believers to persevere in the Christian life. Thus Grace is not merely an initiatory act of God that secures the believer's eternal salvation, but also that which maintains it throughout the entirety of the Christian's life. It is used as a token or proof of salvation, see 2nd Corinthians 1:5. Grace, then, is intrinsically, the capacity for the reception of Divine life, see 1st Peter 1:10.

THE TEN COMMANDMENTS

Exodus 20:3-17

The Ten Commandments are a transcript of the character of God. ~Romans 7:12{NASB}~ states, "So then, the Law is holy, and the commandment is holy and righteous and good." ~Isaiah 6:3{NASB}~ states, "And one called to another and said: 'Holy, holy, holy is the Lord of hosts; the whole earth is full of his glory." John 4:22-24 tells us that God is Spirit; quoting now from ~John 4:22-24{NASB}~ states, "You worship that which you do not know; we worship that which we know, for salvation if from the Jews. But an hour is coming, and now is, when the true worshipers shall worship the Father in spirit and truth; for such people the Father seeks to be His worshipers. God is spirit, and those who worship Him must worship in spirit and truth." The reason of all this is found in the determining statement: God is Spirit; God is Light; God is Love. The predication involves much; that God is personal, and much else. But primarily it indicates that God is not corporeal, and therefore needs no temple. Rarely is the fundamental fact of God's spirituality carried to all its conclusions. The same Greek word used in this text for Spirit, Pneuma, is the word used for the spirit of humanity. The soul, Greek Psuche, is humanities horizontal window, which enables them to be conscious of their environment, their surroundings. All animals, dogs, cats, cattle, horses etc. have souls, meaning they're aware of their surroundings. The spirit is defined as the immaterial part of humanity, the part that is the element of faith. The spirit is what gives humanity the ability to think about God, and is their vertical window. Romans 7:14{NASB} states, "For we know that the Law is spiritual; but I am of flesh, sold into bondage to sin." The idea here is emphatically differentiating between the spiritual and animalistic. Greek Pneumatikos spiritual is the direct opposite of Greek Psuchikos, man with their sinful propensities ruling them.

God, Himself, is the embodiment of perfection, which means that His Law is perfect as well. ~2nd Samuel 22:31{KJV}~ states, "As for God, his way is perfect; the word of the Lord is tried: he is a buckler to all them that trust in him." ~Psalm 119:96{NASB}~ states, "I have seen a limit to all perfection; Thy commandment is exceedingly broad." God's very nature is love, as ~1st John 4:8{NASB}~ states, "The one who does not love does not know God, for God is love." God's perfect law is the culmination of that love, as ~Romans 13:10{NASB}~ states, "Love does no wrong to a neighbor; love therefore is the fulfillment of the law." This means that if we love our neighbor, we will treat them as Christ has dictated in the last six of the Ten Commandments. Also if we love God, we will treat Him as dictated in the first four of the Ten Commandments. Jesus, Himself, was asked about the greatest commandment. "But when the Pharisees heard that He had put the Sadducees to silence, they gathered themselves together. And one of them, a lawyer, asked Him a question, testing Him, 'Teacher, which is the great commandment in the Law?' And He said to him, 'You shall love the Lord your God with all your heart, and with all your soul, and with all your mind. This is the great and foremost commandment. The second is like it, you shall love your neighbor as yourself. On these two commandments depend the whole Law and the Prophets.'" ~Matthew 22:34-40{NASB}~

God is eternal or everlasting, and so is His law. "The eternal God is thy refuge, and underneath are the everlasting arms: and he shall thrust out the enemy from before thee; and shall say destroy them." ~Deuteronomy 33:27{KJV}~ "They are upheld forever and ever; they are performed in truth and uprightness." ~Psalm 111:8{NASB}~ "Do not think that I came to abolish the Law or the Prophets; I did not come to abolish, but to fulfill. For truly I say to you, until heaven and earth pass away, not the smallest letter or stroke shall pass away from the Law, until all is accomplished. Whoever then annuls one of the least of these commandments, and so teaches others, shall be called least in the kingdom of heaven; but whoever keeps and teaches them, he shall be called great in the kingdom of heaven." ~Matthew 5:17-19{NASB}~ "But it is easier for heaven and earth to pass away than for one stroke of a letter of the Law to fail." ~Luke 16:17{NASB}~

The Ten Commandment law controls our moral lives. The first four control our relationship to God, and the last six regulate our relationships with each other, see Exodus 20:3-17 where the Ten Commandments are listed. See also Matthew 19:16-22, the story of the rich young ruler. Also see Matthew 22:34-38, the story of Jesus' interaction with the Pharisees concerning the greatest commandment. The Ten Commandments are binding upon all of humanity. "The conclusion, when all has been heard, is: fear God and keep His commandments, because this applies to every person. For God will bring every act to judgment, everything which is hidden, whether it is good or evil." ~Ecclesiastes 12:13-14{NASB}~ "Now we know that whatever the Law says, it speaks to those who are under the Law, that every mouth may be closed, and all the world may become accountable to God." ~Romans 3:19{NASB}~

There is a large amount of controversy in Christianity concerning the Ten Commandments, as some advocate that the Ten Commandments were strictly Jewish, and were abolished by Christ at the cross. Others advocate that the Ten Commandments are binding upon Christ, but He transferred the obligation of the fourth commandment to the keeping of the first day of the week. Our attitude toward the Law of the Ten Commandments must be the same as Christ's. "I delight to do Thy will, O my God; Thy Law is within my heart." ~Psalm 40:8{NASB}~ This text tells us that Christ had the Ten Commandments in His heart. Christ came into this world to magnify the Law and make it honorable. "The Lord was pleased for His righteousness sake to make the law great and glorious." ~Isaiah 42:21{NASB}~ See also Matthew 5:17-48.

Christ warns us against the foolishness of believing that He had come to abolish the Law. "Do not think that I came to abolish the Law or the Prophets; I did not come to abolish, but to fulfill. For truly I say to you, until heaven and earth pass away, not the smallest letter or stroke shall pass away from the Law, until all is accomplished. Whoever then annuls one of the least of these commandments, and so teaches others, shall be called least in the kingdom of heaven; but whoever keeps and teaches them, he shall be called great in the kingdom of heaven." ~Matthew 5:17-19{NASB}~ Any who believe, teach or preach that Christ set aside God's Law after reading Matthew 5:17-19, are in denial and guilty of willful ignorance.

The Ten Commandments and the plan of salvation (the gospel) are twins and it's impossible to separate them. God's Law exposes sin and convicts sinners. "Because by the works of the Law no flesh will be justified in His sight; for through the Law comes the knowledge of sin." ~Romans 3:20{NASB}~ "What shall we say then? Is the Law sin? May it never be! On the contrary, I would not have come to know sin except through the Law; for I would not have known about coveting if the Law had not said 'You shall not covet...And I was once alive apart from the Law; but when the commandment came, sin became alive, and I died; and this commandment, which was to result in life, proved to result in death for me; for sin, taking opportunity through the commandment, deceived me, and through it killed me. So then, the Law is holy, and the commandment is holy and righteous and good. Therefore did that which is good become a cause of death for me? May it never be! Rather it was sin, in order that it might be shown to be sin by effecting my death through that which is good, that through the commandment sin might become utterly sinful." ~Romans 7:7, 9-13{NASB}~ "Whosoever committeth sin transgresseth also the law: for sin is the transgression of the law." ~1ˢᵗ John 3:4{KJV}~

Where there is no law, there is no transgression, "For the law brings about wrath, but where there is no law, neither is there violation." Romans 4:15{NASB}~ "For until the Law sin was in the world; but sin is not imputed when there is no law." Romans 5:13{NASB}~ It is the gospel of Jesus Christ that offers deliverance from sin. "For I am not ashamed of the gospel, for it is the power of God for salvation to everyone who believes, to the Jew first and also to the Greek." Romans 1:16{NASB}~ "And there is salvation in no one else; for there is no other name under heaven that has been given among men, by which we must be saved." Acts 4:12{NASB}~

"And she will bear a son; and you shall call His name Jesus, for it is He who will save His people from their sins." Matthew 1:21{NASB}~

The new and everlasting covenant provides for the law of the Ten Commandments to be engraved upon the tables of our hearts. "And the Holy Spirit also bears witness to us; for after saying, 'This is the covenant that I will make with them after those days, says the Lord: I will put my laws upon their hearts, and upon their minds write them.'" ~Hebrews 10:15-16{NASB}~ "'Behold, days are coming,' declares the Lord, 'when I will make a new covenant with the house of Israel and with the house of Judah, not like the covenant which I made with their fathers in the day I took them by the hand to bring them out of the land of Egypt, My covenant which they broke, although I was a husband to them,' declares the Lord. 'But this is the covenant which I will make with the house of Israel after those days,' declares the Lord, 'I will put My law within them, and on their heart I will write it; and I will be their God, and they shall be My people.'" ~Jeremiah 31:31-33{NASB}~

The eternal basis of the Ten Commandment laws are based upon the two great commandments of love: "Jesus said unto him, Thou shalt love the Lord thy God with all thy heart, and with all thy soul, and with all thy mind. This is the first and great commandment. And the second is like unto it, Thou shalt love thy neighbor as thyself. On these two commandments hang all the law and the prophets. While the Pharisees were gathered together, Jesus asked them, saying, what think ye of Christ? Whose son is he? They say unto him, 'The son of David.'" ~Matthew 22:37-42{KJV}~ The Ten Commandments are based on the golden rule stated by Christ, "Therefore, however you want people to treat you, so treat them, for this is the Law and the Prophets." ~Matthew 7:12{NASB}~ It is impossible to truly obey the golden rule and be inclined to break one of the Ten Commandments, as Scripture states, "If you love Me, you will keep My commandments." ~John 14:15{NASB}~ "If you keep My commandments, you will abide in My love; just as I have kept My Father's commandments, and abide in His love." ~John 15:10{NASB}~ "The one who says,, 'I have come to know Him, and does not keep His commandments, is a liar, and the truth is not in him; but whoever keeps

His word, in him the love of God has truly been perfected. By this we know that we are in Him: the one who says he abides in Him ought himself to walk in the same manner as He walked. Beloved, I am not writing a new commandment to you, but an old commandment which you have had from the beginning; the old commandment is the word which you have heard." 1ˢᵗ John 2:4-7{NASB}~

The attitude Christian believers have concerning the Ten Commandments are crucial. They delight in it, "For I joyfully concur with the law of God in the inner man." ~Romans 7:22{NASB}~ They establish them by obeying them, "Do we then nullify the Law through faith? May it never be! On the contrary, we establish the Law." ~Romans 3:31(NASB}~ They uphold the teachings of the Law of God in their teaching and their lives. "But prove yourselves doers of the word, and not merely hearers who delude themselves. For if anyone is a hearer of the word and not a doer, he is like a man who looks at his natural face in a mirror; for once he has looked at himself and gone away, he has immediately forgotten what kind of person he was." ~James 1:22-24{NASB}~ see also 1ˢᵗ John 2:4-7. "And the dragon was enraged with the women, and went off to make war with the rest of her offspring, who keep the commandments of God and hold to the testimony of Jesus." ~Revelation 12:17{NASB}~ "Here is the perseverance of the saints who keep the commandments of God and their faith in Jesus." ~Revelation 14:12{NASB}~

Being that the Ten Commandments are an expression of God's character, it follows that those who work against God's law are, in fact, enemies of God. "Because the mind set on the flesh is hostile toward God; for it does not subject itself to the law of God, for it is not even able to do so." ~Romans 8:7{NASB}~ "Can a throne of destruction be allied with Thee, one which devises mischief by decree?" ~Psalm 94:20{NASB}~ God accuses them of being liars. "Now go, write it on a tablet before them and inscribe it on a scroll, that it may serve in the time to come as a witness forever. For this is a rebellious people, false sons, sons who refuse to listen to the instruction of the Lord." ~Isaiah 30:8-9{NASB}~ "Everyone who practices sin also practices lawlessness; and sin is lawlessness." ~1ˢᵗ John 3:4{NASB}~

There are wonderful promises made to those who love the laws of God. They have great peace. "Those who love Thy law have great peace, and nothing causes them to stumble." ~Psalm 119:165{NASB}~ "If only you had paid attention to My commandments! Then your well-being would have been like a river, and your righteousness like the waves of the sea." ~Isaiah 48:18{NASB}~ They will have prosperity, see Psalm 1. They will have right to the tree of life. "Blessed are those who wash their robes, that they may have the right to the tree of life, and may enter by the gates into the city." ~Revelation 22:14{NASB}~

THE CREATION SABBATH

Genesis 2:2-3

It is noteworthy and thought provoking that God chose to create this world in six evening and morning days, see Genesis 1:5, 8, 13, 19, 23, & 31. The creations days were from even unto even as ~Leviticus 23:32{NASB}~ states, "It is to be a sabbath of complete rest to you, and you shall humble your souls; on the ninth of the month at evening, from evening until evening you shall keep your sabbath." From sunset to sunset as ~Mark 1:32{NASB}~ states, "And when evening had come, after the sun had set, the began bringing to Him all who were ill and those demon possessed." Also ~Deuteronomy 16:6{NASB}~ states, "But at the place where the Lord your God chooses to establish His name, you will sacrifice the Passover in the evening at sunset, at the time that you came out of Egypt."

How God created the world contrasted by the theory of evolution. God spoke the world into being, see Genesis 1:3, 6, 9, 11, 14, 15, 20, 24, 26; & ~Psalm 148:5{NASB}~ which states, "Let them praise the name of the Lord, for He commanded and they were created." The creation week consisted of six evening and morning days. Why would God utilize this method when He could have simply spoken the world and everything in it into existence in a moment, in the twinkling of an eye, so to speak? But God, in His infinite wisdom, took six twenty-four-hour days to complete creation. God, who knows the end from the beginning chose to measure time in this manner. ~Acts 15:18{NASB}~ states, "Says the Lord, who makes these things known from of old."

God created the world in six days and He rested the seventh day, thus setting an eternal precedent to be followed by all humanity. ~Exodus 20:8-11{NASB}~ states, "Remember the sabbath day, to keep it holy. Six days you shall labor and do all your work, but the seventh day is a sabbath of the Lord your God; in it you shall not do any work, you are your son or your daughter, your male or your female servant or your cattle or your sojourner who stays with you. For in six days the Lord made the heavens and the earth, the sea and all that is in them, and rested on the seventh day; therefore the Lord blessed the sabbath day and made it holy." ~Hebrews 4:9-10{NASB}~ states, "There remains therefore a Sabbath rest for the people of God. For the one who has entered His rest has himself also rested from his works, as God did His." That fact alone makes the seventh day of the week God's rest day forever. ~Ecclesiastes 3:14{NASB}~ states, "I know that everything God does will remain forever; there is nothing to add to it and there is nothing to take from it, for God has so worked that men should fear Him."

The rest of the Creator on the seventh day marks the beginning of our perpetual weekly cycle. This is a fact to keep in mind as we study the creation Sabbath. The weekly cycle is measured by the Sabbath. Compare with me the following: ~Exodus 16:3-28{NASB}~ states, "The sons of Israel said to them, "Would that we had died by the Lord's hand in the land of Egypt, when we sat by the pots of meat, when we ate bread to the full; for you have brought us out into this wilderness to kill this whole assembly with hunger." Then the Lord said to Moses, "Behold, I will rain bread from heaven for you; and the people shall go out and gather a day's portion every day, that I may test them, whether or not they will walk in My instruction. On the sixth day, when they prepare what they bring in, it will be twice as much as they gather daily." So Moses and Aaron said to all the sons of Israel, "At evening you will know that the Lord has brought you out of the land of Egypt; and in the morning you will see the glory of the Lord, for He hears your grumblings against the Lord; and what are we, that you grumble against us?" Moses said, "This will happen when the Lord gives you meat to eat in the evening, and bread to the full in the morning; for the Lord hears your grumblings which you grumble against Him. And what are we? Your grumblings are not against us but against the Lord." Then Moses said to Aaron, "Say to all the congregation of the sons of Israel, 'Come near before the Lord, for He has heard your grumblings.'" It came about as Aaron spoke to the whole congregation of the sons of Israel, that they looked toward the wilderness, and behold, the glory of the Lord appeared in the cloud. And the Lord spoke to Moses, saying, "I have heard the grumblings of the sons of Israel; speak to them, saying, 'At twilight you shall eat meat, and in the morning you shall be filled with bread; and you shall know that I am the Lord your God.'" So it came about at evening that the quails came up and covered the camp, and in the morning there was a layer of dew around the camp. When the layer of dew evaporated, behold, on the surface of the wilderness there was a fine flake-like thing, fine as the frost on the ground. When the sons of Israel saw it, they said to one another, "What is it?" For they did not know what it was. And Moses said to them, "It is the bread which the Lord has given you to eat. This is what the Lord has commanded, 'Gather of it every man as much as he should eat; you shall take an omer apiece according to the number of persons each of you has in his tent.'" The sons of Israel did so, and some gathered much and some little. When they measured it with an omer, he who had gathered much had no excess, and he who had gathered little had no lack; every man gathered as much as he should eat. Moses said to them, "Let no man leave any of it until morning." But they did not listen to Moses, and some left part of it until morning, and it bred worms and became foul; and Moses was angry with them. They gathered it morning by morning, every man as much as he should eat; but when the sun grew hot, it would melt. Now on the sixth day they gathered twice as much bread, two omers for each one. When all the leaders of the congregation came and told Moses, then he said to them, "This is what the Lord meant: Tomorrow is a sabbath observance, a holy sabbath to the Lord. Bake what you will bake and boil what you will boil, and all that is left over put aside to be kept until morning." So they put it aside until morning, as Moses had ordered, and it did not become foul nor was there any worm in it. Moses said, "Eat it today, for today is a sabbath to the Lord; today you will not find it in the field. Six days you shall gather it, but on the seventh day, the sabbath, there will be none." It came about on the seventh day that some of the people went out to gather, but they found none. Then the Lord said to Moses, "How long do you refuse to keep My commandments and My instructions?"

With ~Ezekiel 46:1{NASB}~ which states, "Thus says the Lord God, 'The gate of the inner court facing east shall be shut the six working days; but it shall be opened on the sabbath day, and opened on the day of the new moon." Also ~Exodus 20:8-11{NASB}~ which states, "Remember the sabbath day, to keep it holy. Six days you shall labor and do all your work, but the seventh day is a sabbath of the Lord your God; in it you shall not do any work, you or your son or your daughter your male or your female servant or your cattle or your sojourner who stays with you." This measure of time has been recognized by humanity since the very beginning of civilization.

The creation Sabbath has as its origin in a threefold act of the creator. God rested on the seventh day from all His work and was refreshed, as ~Genesis 2:3{NASB}~ states, "Then God blessed the seventh day and sanctified it, because in it He rested from all His work which God had created and made." Also ~Exodus 31:17{NASB}~ states, "It is a sign between Me and the sons of Israel forever; for in six days the Lord made heaven and earth, but on the seventh day He ceased from labor, and was refreshed." This fact, alone, makes the seventh day of the week God's holy Sabbath day for ever, as Ecclesiastes 3:14{NASB}~ states, "I know that everything God does will remain forever; there is nothing to add to it and there is nothing to take from it, for God has so worked that men should fear Him." He blessed the seventh day because that in it He had rested from all His works, which God created and made. God's bestowal of His blessing on the seventh day Sabbath gives the lie to the theory that the Sabbath is a burden to those who seek to keep it. Compare, with me, the verse quoted prior Genesis 2:3 with ~1st Chronicles 17:27{NASB}~ which states, "And now it hath pleased Thee to bless the house of Thy servant, that it may continue forever before Thee; for Thou, O Lord, hast blessed, and it is blessed forever." Also ~Numbers 23:20{NASB}~ which states, "Behold I have received a command to bless; when He has blessed, then I cannot revoke it." God hallowed, set aside the seventh day Sabbath, by His own example, "For in six days the Lord made the heavens and the earth, the sea and all that is in them, and rested on the seventh day; therefore the Lord blessed the sabbath day and made it holy." ~Exodus 20:11{NASB}~

God's act when bringing the weekly Sabbath into being at the beginning of creation is Biblical proof that the weekly Sabbath predates sin in this world, and shows that it cannot be nationalized or localized as some would have us think. It predates the Jewish race by over twenty-four hundred years. Please note carefully, with me, why God made the weekly Sabbath. It was made for humanity, as ~Mark 2:27{NASB}~ states, "And He was saying to them, 'The Sabbath was made for man, and not man for the Sabbath." Please note that the Sabbath was made, this fact excludes it from the sabbaths that came into being in the early history of the children of Israel. ~Leviticus 23:4-37{NASB}~'These are the appointed times of the Lord, holy convocations which you shall proclaim at the times appointed for them. In the first month, on the fourteenth day of the month at twilight is the Lord's Passover. Then on the fifteenth day of the same month there is the Feast of Unleavened Bread to the Lord; for seven days you shall eat unleavened bread. On the first day you shall have a holy convocation; you shall not do any laborious work. But for seven days you shall present an offering by fire to the Lord. On the seventh day is a holy convocation; you shall not do any laborious work.'" Then the Lord spoke to Moses, saying, "Speak to the sons of Israel and say to them, 'When you enter the land which I am going to give to you and reap its harvest, then you shall bring in the sheaf of the first fruits of your harvest to the priest. He shall wave the sheaf before the Lord for you to be accepted; on the day after the sabbath the priest shall wave it. Now on the day when you wave the sheaf, you shall offer a male lamb one year old without defect for a burnt offering to the Lord. Its grain offering shall then be two-tenths of an ephah of fine flour mixed with oil, an offering by fire to the Lord for a soothing aroma, with its drink offering, a fourth of a hin of wine. Until this same day, until you have brought in the offering of your God, you shall eat neither bread nor roasted grain nor new growth. It is to be a perpetual statute throughout your generations in all your dwelling places. 'You shall also count for yourselves from the day after the sabbath, from the day when you brought in the sheaf of the wave offering; there shall be seven complete sabbaths. You shall count fifty days to the day after the seventh sabbath; then you shall present a new grain offering to the Lord. You shall bring in from your dwelling places two loaves of bread for a wave offering, made of two-tenths of an ephah; they shall be of a fine flour, baked with leaven as first fruits to the Lord. Along with the bread you shall present seven one year old male lambs without defect, and a bull of the herd and two rams; they are to be a burnt offering to the Lord, with their grain offering and their drink offerings, an offering by fire of a soothing aroma to the Lord. You shall also offer one male goat for a sin offering and two male lambs one year old for a sacrifice of peace offerings. The priest shall then wave them with the bread of the first fruits for a wave offering with two lambs before the Lord; they are to be holy to the Lord for the priest. On this same day you shall make a proclamation as well; you are to have a holy convocation. You shall do no laborious work. It is to be a perpetual statute in all your dwelling places throughout your generations. 'When you reap the harvest of your land, moreover, you shall not reap to the very corners of your field nor gather the gleaning of your harvest; you are to leave them for the needy and the alien. I am the Lord your God."' Again the Lord spoke to Moses, saying, "Speak to the sons of Israel, saying, 'In the seventh month on the first of the month you shall have a rest, a reminder by blowing of trumpets, a holy convocation. You shall not do any laborious work, but you shall present an offering by fire to the Lord."' The Lord spoke to Moses, saying, "On exactly the tenth day of this seventh month is the Day of Atonement; it shall be a holy convocation for you, and you shall humble your souls and present an offering by fire to the Lord. You shall not do any work on this same day, for it is a day of atonement, to make atonement on your behalf before the Lord your God. If there is any person who will not humble himself on this same day, he shall be cut off from his people. As for any person who does any work on this same day, that person I will destroy from among his people. You shall do no work at all. It is to be a perpetual statute throughout your generations in all your dwelling places. It is to be a sabbath of complete rest to you, and you shall humble your souls; on the ninth of the month at evening, from evening until evening you shall keep your sabbath." Again the Lord spoke to Moses, saying, "Speak to the sons of Israel, saying, 'On the fifteenth of this seventh month is the Feast of Booths for seven days to the Lord. On the first day is a holy convocation; you shall do no laborious work of any kind. For seven days you shall present an offering by fire to the Lord. On the eighth day you shall have a holy convocation and present an offering by fire to the Lord; it is an assembly. You shall do no laborious work. 'These are the appointed times of the Lord which you shall proclaim as holy convocations, to present offerings by fire to the Lord—burnt offerings and grain offerings, sacrifices and drink offerings, each day's matter on its own day."

It was made, they were appointed. It was made for humanity, the entire human race, as ~Mark 2:27-28{NASB}~ states, "And He was saying to them, 'The Sabbath was made for man, and not man for the Sabbath, consequently, the Son of Man is Lord even of the Sabbath." That fact makes it a universal institution dating back to creation.

WHEN SATAN COMES OUT AHEAD

Mark 9:14-29

The ministry of Christ, in this world, is twofold. ~Luke 19:10{NASB}~ states, "For the Son of Man has come to seek and save that which was lost." Christ came to call, not the righteous, but sinners, as ~Luke 15:7{NASB}~ states, "I tell you that in the same way, there will be more joy in heaven over one sinner who repents, than over ninety-nine righteous persons who need no repentance." That, of course, includes each and every one of us. ~Isaiah 53:6{NASB}~ states, "All of us like sheep have gone astray, each of us has turned to his own way; but the Lord has caused the iniquity of us all to fall on Him." Also 1st Peter 2:25{NASB}~ states, "For you were continually straying like sheep, but now you have returned to the Shepherd and Guardian of your souls."

But Christ also came to train workers for the work of the gospel. This is readily evident that in most of His ministry He always took some of His disciples into His daily ministry, see Mark 9:14-29 which gives a vivid illustration of this training for His disciples. Quoting now ~Mark 9:14-23{NASB}~ which states, "And when they came back to the disciples, they saw a large crowd around them, and some scribes arguing with them. And immediately, when the entire crowd saw Him, they were amazed, and began running up to greet Him. And He asked them, 'What are you discussing with them?' and one of the crowd answered Him, 'Teacher, I brought You my son, possessed with a spirit which makes him mute; and whenever it seizes him, it dashes him to the ground and he foams at the mouth, and grinds his teeth, and stiffens out. And I told Your disciples to cast it out, and they could not do it.' And He answered them and said, 'O unbelieving generation, how long shall I be with you? How long shall I put up with you? Bring him to Me!' And they brought the boy to Him. And when he saw Him, immediately the spirit threw him into a convulsion, and falling to the ground, he began rolling about and foaming at the mouth. And He asked his father, 'How long has this been happening to him?' and he said, 'from childhood. And it has often thrown him both into the fire and into the water to destroy him. But if You can do anything, take pity on us and help us!' And Jesus said to him, 'If You can! All things are possible to him who believes.' Immediately the boy's father cried out began saying, 'I do believe; help my unbelief.' And when Jesus saw that a crowd was rapidly gathering, He rebuked the unclean spirit, saying to it, 'You deaf and dumb spirit, I command you, come out of him and do not enter him again.' And after crying out and throwing him into terrible convulsions, it came out; and the boy became so much like a corpse that most of them said, 'He is dead!' But Jesus took him by the hand and raised him; and he got up. And when He had come into the house, His disciples began questioning Him privately, 'Why could we not cast it out?' And He said to them, 'This kind cannot come out by anything but prayer.'"

Mark 9:14-20 also brings to our minds a dual scene. Christ's mountain top glory as denoted in ~Matthew 17:1-5{NASB}~ which states, "And six days later Jesus took with Him Peter and James and John his brother, and brought them up to a high mountain by themselves. And He was transfigured before them; and His face shone like the sun, and His garments became as which as light. And behold, Moses and Elijah appeared to them, talking with Him. And Peter answered and said to Jesus, 'Lord, it is good for us to be here; if You wish, I will make three tabernacles here, one for You, and one for Moses, and one for Elijah.' While he was still speaking, behold, a bright clouds overshadowed them; and behold, a voice out of the cloud saying, 'This is My beloved Son, with whom I am well-pleased; listen to Him.'"

The transfiguration of Christ. Can you imagine what it must have been like for the disciples!? It gave them a preview of the coming glory in Christ's kingdom. The three disciples became so enchanted by the divine panorama that they would have continued there. Little did they sense the gloom and frustration of their fellow disciples at the foot of the mountain. A different scene is unfolding when they leave the mount of Transfiguration and re-enter the valley below. There they see a devil-plagued child, along with a perplexed father, and a group of defeated and disillusioned disciples, see again Mark 9:14-29. This scene is quite typical of the modern Disciples of Christ. Some have themselves, also experienced mountain top experiences, while their brethren have experienced defeat because of sin in their lives. Worldliness, in one form or another, keeps them powerless to cope with ever present problems of their Christian profession.

When Satan comes out ahead. The afflicted boy in ~Mark 9:18-19{NASB}, which states, "And whenever it seizes him, it dashes him to the ground and he foams at the mouth, and grinds his teeth, and stiffens out. And I told Your disciples to cast it out, and they could not do it. And He answered them and said, 'O unbelieving generation, how long shall I be with you? How long shall I put up with you? Bring him to Me!." Or the troubled father in ~Mark 9:17-18{NASB}~ which states, "And one of the crowd answered Him, 'Teacher, I brought You my son, possessed with a spirit which makes him mute; and whenever it seizes him, it dashes him to the ground and he foams at the mouth, and grinds his teeth, and stiffens out. And I told Your disciples to cast it out, and they could not do it." The perplexed and defeated disciples, as the multitudes had pressed them for action to prove their connection with God. Their heart condition was such that they were woefully unprepared for their mission. They had been separated from their Master, and spent much of their time in faultfinding with each other.

This is a special lesson for modern Israel. In the school of Christ we find that God leads His people in mysterious ways. He invites us to see and taste the glory of things to come. ~1st Corinthians 2:9-11{NASB}~ states, "But just as it is written, 'things which eye has not seen and ear has not heard, and which have not entered the heart of man, all that God has prepared for those who love Him. For to us God revealed them through the Spirit; for the Spirit searches all things, even the depths of God. For who among men knows the thoughts of a man except the spirit of the man, which is in him? Even so the thoughts of God no one knows except the Spirit of God.'"

We are, at times, enchanted by the glory that is portrayed in Bible Prophecy. The scene before us helps us to forget, for the time being, the trials and disappointments of the everyday life. That is one of God's ways to encourage us in our experience. Even the Son of God was strengthened, by the joy that was set before him, to take the cup of suffering that faced Him. ~Hebrews 12:2{NASB}~ states, "Fixing our eyes on Jesus, the author and perfecter of faith, who for the joy set before Him endured the cross, despising the shame, and has sat down at the right hand of the throne of God." But there is another side of our opening text, we are not ready to continue in the rapture of heavenly glory. There are souls to save; they are waiting for us to bring them the message of salvation. We have work to do. ~John 9:4{NASB}~ states, "We must work the works of Him who sent Me, as long as it is day; night is coming, when no man can work." Now is the time for labor, we must not be indolent workers, but, being aware that the night is soon coming, when we no longer will be able to work for Christ.

Of special importance for us is that whenever we become involved in our sinful pleasures, Satan comes out ahead; he uses our weakness to hinder the work of God. That is, I believe, one of the primary lessons to be gathered from our opening text. Whenever we become separated from the Lord, we lose connection with the power to win against Satan and sin. Fasting and prayer, according to the words of Christ, are the key to power to become useful in the cause of soul winning.

The Theory of a Secret Rapture

The theory of a secret rapture is a popular theory concerning the object of Christ's second coming. According to this theory, Christ will come in secret. Matthew 24:44{NASB} states, "For this reason you be ready too; for the Son of Man is coming at an hour when you do not think He will." Two of the main components of this theory are, two will be sleeping in the same bed, and one will be taken away, without the other knowing anything about it, and b. the bride of the Lamb, which is the church, will be snatched away in a rapture, while the rest of the world continues on as usual. It is then, according to this theory, that the anti-christ will begin his reign on the earth. According to this theory, a. he, the anti-christ will cause all humanity to receive his mark; while those who refuse the mark, will experience great tribulation, and b. Christ will begin His reign upon the earth for a thousand years in old Jerusalem; and then the Jews will see that they had been wrong in crucifying Him, and will, at that time, accept Him as their savior.

In light of this information, it is critical that we examine several Biblical facts concerning the appearing of the Son of Man, and its effect upon the world. 1. Christ's coming will not be secret by any stretch of the imagination, as ~Revelation 1:7{NASB}~ states, "Behold, He is coming with the clouds, and every eye will see Him, even those who pierced Him; and all tribes of the earth will mourn over him. Even so. Amen." 2. The living wicked will seek shelter from the rocks and beneath the mountains from Christ. ~Revelation 6:15-17{NASB}~ states, "And the kings of the earth and the great men and the commanders and the rich and the strong and every slave and free man, hid themselves in the caves and among the rocks of the mountains; and they said to the mountains and to the rocks, 'Fall on us and hid us from the presence of Him who sits on the throne, and from the wrath of the Lamb; for the great day of their wrath has come; and who is able to stand?" 3. Christ will come with a shout that awakens the dead. ~John 5:28-29{NASB}~ states, "Do not marvel at this; for an hour is coming, in which all who are in the tombs shall hear His voice, and shall come forth; those who did the good deeds to a resurrection of life, those who committed the evil deeds to a resurrection of judgment." ~Matthew 16:27{NASB}~ states, "For the Son of Man is going to come in the glory of His father with His angels; and will then recompense every man according to his deeds." ~Matthew 24:30{NASB}~ states, "And then the sign of the Son of Man will appear in the sky, and then all the tribes of the earth will mourn, and they will see the Son of Man coming in the clouds of the sky with power and great glory." 1st Thessalonians 4:16{KJV} states, "For the Lord himself shall descend from heaven with a shout, with the voice of the archangel, and with the trump of God: and the dead in Christ shall rise first."

There will not be a time frame for second chances, as the story of the ten virgins denoted in Matthew 25:1-12 details. The bitter disappointment that will come to those who believe and accept the second chance theory. Luke 13:24-28{NASB} states, "Strive to enter by the narrow door; for many, I tell you, will seek to enter and will not be able. Once the head of the house gets up and shuts the door, and you begin to stand outside and knock on the door, saying, 'Lord, open up to us!' then He will answer and say to you, I do not know where you are from. Then you will begin to say, 'We ate and drank in Your presence, and You taught in our streets' and He will say, 'I tell you, I do not know where you are from; depart from Me, all you evildoers.' There will be weeping and gnashing of teeth there when you see Abraham and Isaac and Jacob and all the prophets in the kingdom of God, but yourselves being cast out." The time for salvation is now. ~2nd Corinthians 6:1-3{NASB} states, "And working together with Him, we also urge you not to receive the grace of God in vain—for He says, 'at the acceptable time I listened to you, and on the day of salvation I helped you'; behold, now is the acceptable time,' behold now is the day of salvation'—giving no cause for offense in anything, in order that the ministry be not discredited.'" ~John 9:4{KJV}~ states, "I must work the works of him that sent me, while it is day: the night cometh, when no man can work." & ~Hebrews 3:7-9{NASB}~ states, "Therefore, just as the Holy Spirit says, 'Today if you hear His voice, do not harden your hearts as when they provoked Me, as in the day of trial in the wilderness where your fathers tried Me by testing Me, and say My works for forty years.'" The gospel of the kingdom, which is now going to all nations, will be preached before probation ends; then the end is come, and no other opportunity for salvation is open as ~Matthew 24:14{NASB}~ states, "And this gospel of the kingdom shall be preached in the whole world for a witness to all the nations, and then the end shall come."

The following events will mark the second coming of Christ: 1. The righteous will be immortalized. ~1st Corinthians 15:50-57{NASB}~ states, "Now I say this, brethren, that flesh and blood cannot inherit the kingdom of God; nor does the perishable inherit the imperishable. Behold, I tell you a mystery; we shall not all sleep, but we shall all be changed, in a moment, in the twinkling of an eye, at the last trumpet; for the trumpet will sound, and the dead will be raised imperishable, and we shall be changed. For this imperishable must put on the imperishable, and this mortal must put on immortality. But when this perishable will have put on the imperishable, and this mortal will have put on immortality, then will come about the saying that is written, 'Death is swallowed up in victory, O death, where is your victory? O death, where is your sting?' The sting of death is sin, and the power of sin is the law; but thanks be to God, who gives us the victory through our Lord Jesus Christ. Therefore, my beloved brethren, be steadfast, immovable, always abounding in the work of the Lord, knowing that your toil is not in vain in the Lord." ~Mark 10:28-30{NASB}~ states, "Peter began to say to Him, 'Behold, we have left everything and followed You.' Jesus said, 'Truly I say to you, there is no one who has left house or brothers or sisters or mother or father or children or farms, for My sake and for the gospel's sake, but that he shall receive a hundred times as much now in the present age, houses and brothers and sisters and mothers and children and farms, along with persecutions; and in the age to come, eternal life.'" ~John 5:28-29{NASB}~ states, "Do not marvel at this; for an hour is coming, in which all who are in the tombs will hear his voice, and shall come forth, those who did good deeds to a resurrection of life, and those who committed the evil deeds to the resurrection of judgment." & Daniel 12:2-3{KJV} states, "And many of them that sleep in the dust of the earth shall awake, some to everlasting life, and some to shame and everlasting contempt. And they that be wise shall shine as the brightness of the firmament; and they that turn many to righteousness as the stars for ever and ever."

2. The righteous will be removed from this planet. ~John 14:1-3{NASB}~ states, "Let not your heart be troubled; believe in God, believe also in Me. In My Father's house are many dwelling places; if it were not so, I would have told you; for I go to prepare a place for you. And if I go and prepare a place for you, I will come again, and receive you to Myself; that where I am, there you may be also." ~1st Thessalonians 4:13-17{NASB}~ states, "But we do not want you to be uninformed, brethren, about those who are asleep, that you may not grieve, as do the rest who have no hope. For if we believe that Jesus died and rose again, even so God will bring with Him those who have fallen asleep in Jesus. For this we say to you by the word of the Lord, that we who are alive, and remain until the coming of the Lord, shall not precede those who have fallen asleep. For the Lord Himself will descend from heaven with a shout, with the voice of the archangel, and with the trumpet of God; and the dead in Christ shall rise first. Then we who are alive and remain shall be caught up together with them in the clouds to meet the Lord in the air, and thus we shall always be with the Lord." ~Revelation 4:6{NASB}~ states, "And before the throne there was, as it were, a sea of glass like crystal; and in the center and round the throne, four living creatures full of eyes in front and behind." & ~Revelation 15:1-3{NASB}~ states, "And I saw another sign in heaven, great and marvelous, seven angels who had seven plagues, which are the last, because in them the wrath of God is finished. And I saw, as it were, a sea of glass mixed with fire, and those who had come off victorious from the beast and from his image and from the number of his name, standing on the sea of glass, holding harps of God. And they sang the song of Moses the bond-servant of God and the song of the Lamb, saying, 'Great and marvelous are Thy works, O Lord God, the Almighty; righteous and true are Thy ways, Thou King of the nations."

The living wicked will be slain by the breath of the mouth of the Son of God. ~2nd Thessalonians 1:7-8{NASB}~ states, "And to give relief to you who are afflicted and to us as well when the Lord Jesus shall be revealed from heaven with His mighty angels in flaming fire, dealing out retribution to those who do not know God and to those who do not obey the gospel of our Lord Jesus." ~2nd Thessalonians 2:9-11{NASB}~ states, "That is, the one whose coming is in accord with the activity of Satan, and with all power and signs and false wonders, and with all the deception of wickedness for those who perish, because they did not receive the love of the truth so as to be saved. And for this reason God will send upon them a deluding influence so that they might believe what is false." ~Isaiah 11:4{NASB}~ states, "But with righteousness He will judge the poor, and decide with fairness for the afflicted of the earth; and He will strike the earth with the rod of His mouth, and with the breath of His lips He will slay the wicked." & ~Revelation 19:15{KJV}~ states, "And out of his mouth goeth a sharp sword, that with it he should smite the nations: and he shall rule them with a rod of iron: and he treadeth the winepress of the fierceness and wrath of Almighty God." There will be no living creature, which includes human beings, on this earth after the second coming of Christ for the space of one thousand years. ~Jeremiah 4:25{NASB}~ states, "I looked, and behold, there was no man, and all the birds of the heavens had fled." & ~Jeremiah 25:34-38{NASB}~ states, "Wail, you shepherds, and cry; and wallow in ashes, you masters of the flock; hear the sound of the cry of the shepherds, and the ailing of the masters of the flock! For the Lord is destroying their pasture, and the peaceful folds are made silent because of the fierce anger of the Lord. He has left His hiding place like the lion; for their land has become a horror because of the fierceness of the oppressing sword, and because of His fierce anger." The earth will not be suitable for human survival. ~Isaiah 24:17-30{NASB}~ states, "Terror, and pit and snare confront you, O inhabitant of the earth. Then it will be he who flees at the report of disaster will fall into the pit, and he who climbs out of the pit shall be caught in the snare. For the windows above are opened, and the foundations of the earth shake. The earth is broken asunder, the earth is split through, the earth is shaken violently. The earth reels to and fro like a drunkard, and it totters like a shack, for its transgression is heavy upon it, and it will fall, never to rise again. So it will happen in that day, the Lord will punish the host of heaven, on high, and the kings of the earth, on earth. And they will be gathered together like prisoners in the dungeon, and will be confined in a prison, and after many days they will be punished. Then the moon will be abashed, and the sun ashamed; for the Lord of hosts will reign on Mount Zion in Jerusalem, and His glory will be before his elders."

Just before the Lord comes, the people who have been deceived by the false shepherds will turn upon them with all the fury to destroy them, and the false preachers themselves will weep because God will destroy their pasture. ~Isaiah 56:9-12{NASB}~ states, "All you beasts of the field, all you beasts in the forest, come to eat. His watchman are blind, all of them know nothing. All of them are dumb dogs unable to bark, dreamers lying down, who love to slumber; and the dogs are greedy, they are not satisfied. And they are shepherds who have no understanding; they have all turned to their own way, each one to his unjust gain, to the last one. 'Come,' they say, 'let us get wine, and let us drink heavily of strong drink; and tomorrow will be like today, only more so." & ~Jeremiah 25:34-38{NASB}~ states, "'Wail, you shepherds, and cry; and wallow in ashes, you masters of the flock for the days of your slaughter and your dispersions have come, and you shall fall like a choice vessel. Flight shall perish from the shepherds, and escape from the masters of the flock. Hear the sound of the cry of the shepherds, and the wailing of the masters of the flock! For the Lord is destroying their pasture, and the peaceful folds are made silent because of the fierce anger of the Lord. He has left His hiding place like the lion; for their land has become a horror because of the fierceness of the oppressing sword, and because of His fierce anger.'"

Here are a few Bible facts to keep in mind. 1. The time of probation is now. ~John 9:4{NASB}~ states, "We must work the works of Him who sent Me, as long as it is day; night is coming, when no man can work." ~2nd Corinthians 6:1-3{NASB}~ states, "And working together with Him, we also urge you not to receive the grace of God in vain—for He says, 'At the acceptable time I listened to you, and on the day of salvation I helped you'; behold now is the day of salvation—fiving no cause for offense in anything, in order that the ministry be not discredited." There will be bitter disillusionment for many, who accepted the second chance theory. ~Luke 13:25-28{NASB}~ states, "Once the head of the house gets up and shuts the door, and yo begin to stand outside and knock on the door, saying, 'Lord, open up to us!' then He will answer and say to you, 'I do not know where you are from.' Then you will begin to say, 'we ate and drank in Your presence and You taught in our streets'; and He will say, 'I tell you, I do not know where you are from; depart from Me, all you evildoers.' There will be weeping and gnashing of teeth there when you see Abraham and Isaac and Jacob and all the prophets in the kingdom of God, but yourselves being cast out." ~Matthew 25:12{NASB}~ states, "But he answered and said, 'Truly I say to you, I do not know you.'" & ~Revelation 1:7{NASB}~ states, "Behold, he is coming with the clouds, and every eye will see him, even those who pierced him; and all the tribes of the earth will mourn over him. So shall it be! Amen."

Beware of the so-called secret rapture theory, it is not true; it is false and must be rejected by every truth-loving person. This theory was invented by Satan to keep the minds of men from recognizing the great prophetic truths for our time. Theological claims for this theory gave no Biblical foundation and are intended to keep the people from accepting God's message. To escape these deceptions we must study Present Truth and cleave unto it with all our hearts.

THE STRANGE ACT OF GOD

~Isaiah 28:21{NASB}~ states, "For the Lord will rise up as at mount Perazim, He will be stirred up as in the valley of Gibeon; to do His task, His unusual task, and to work His work, His extraordinary work." This is a very unusual text for the following reasons. 1. God's very nature is love—~1st John 4:8{NASB}~ states, "The one who does not love does not know God, for God is love." 2. God, by His nature, is very longsuffering—~Exodus 34:6{NASB}~ states, "Then the Lord passed by in front of him and proclaimed, 'The Lord, the Lord God, compassionate and gracious, slow to anger, and abounding in lovingkindness and truth." 3. God, by His nature, is merciful and gracious.

By nature, God is merciful, gracious and long-suffering, see the verses denoted prior. It is completely alien to His nature to inflict pain, punishment and death. That being said, God will by no means clear the guilty of wrongdoing, see Exodus 34:7. When humanity sees Christ coming in the clouds of heaven as a warrior to subdue His enemies, see Revelation 19:11-21, they will see Him in a role that appears vastly different then they have ever known prior. The Lamb of God will then appear as ""the Lion of the tribe of Judah" see Revelation 5:5-6{NASB} which states, "And one of the elders said to me, 'Stop weeping; behold, the Lion that is from the tribe of Judah, the root of David, has overcome so as to open the book and its seven seals." And I saw between the throne (with the four living creatures-in Greek Zoon-thinking animals) and the elders a Lamb standing, as if slain, having seven horns and seven eyes, which are the seven Spirits of God, sent out into all the earth.'"

The questions that needs to be answered are the following: 1. What is the strange work He has to do? & 2. What is the strange act the He will bring to pass? God seeks to save sinners—"For God so loved the world, that He gave His only begotten Son, that whoever believes in Him should not perish, but have eternal life. For God did not send the Son into the world to judge the world, but that the world should be saved through Him." ~John 3:16-17{NASB}~ See the following for further study, ~Matthew 18:11{KJV}~ which states, "For the Son of man is come to save that which was lost." & ~Luke 19:10{NASB}~ which states, "For the Son of Man has come to seek and to save that which was Lost." ~2nd Corinthians 5:21{NASB}~ states, "He made Him who knew no sin to be sin on our behalf, that we might become the righteousness of God in Him."

THE STRANGE ACT OF GOD: 1. He will destroy humanity that He had created for His glory. 2. He will cast them that are wicked into the lake of fire and destroy them. (a). "For behold, the day is coming, burning like a furnace; and all the arrogant and every evildoer will be chaff; and the day that is coming will set them ablaze' says the Lord of hosts,, 'so that it will leave them neither root nor branch. But for you who fear My name the sun of righteousness will rise with healing in its wings; and you will go forth and skip about like calves from the stall. And you will tread down the wicked, for they shall be ashes under the soles of your feet on the day which I am preparing,' says the Lord of hosts." ~Malachi 4:1-3{NASB}~ ~Matthew 3:12{NASB}~ states, "And His winnowing fork is in His hand, and He will thoroughly clear His threshing floor; and He will gather His wheat into the barn, but He will burn up the chaff with unquenchable fire."

Why is this act of God so strange? The fires of hell were never intended for any human, but for the devil and his angels. 1. "Then He will also say to those on His left, 'Depart from Me, accursed ones, into the eternal fire which has been prepared for the devil and his angels." ~Matthew 25:41{NASB}~ Man was created for God's glory. 1. "Worthy art Thou, our Lord and our God, to receive glory and honor and power; for Thou didst create all things, and because of thy will they existed, and were created." ~Revelation 4:11{NASB}~ The following facts must be kept in mind, 1.

God did everything he could to save humanity. 2. He set in motion all the power in the universe to seek and to save the lost—including the gift of His one and only Son. (a). "For God so loved the world that he gave his one and only Son, that whoever believes in him shall not perish but have eternal life. For God did not send his Son into the world to condemn the world, but to save the world through him."

There are other points or reasons which make the destruction of the wicked so strange. 1. God is love, and it seems strange for love to destroy. & 2. God gave the very best He had, and that shows that it was very unnatural for Him to destroy that which He had sought to save. Let's take a brief look at the nature of the punishment of the wicked: Scripture says, "For the wages of sin is death, but the free gift of God is eternal life in Christ Jesus our Lord." ~Romans 6:23{NASB}~ In the book of Revelation we read about the "second death." ~Revelation 2:11{NIV}~ states, "He who has an ear, let him hear what the Spirit says to the churches, He who overcomes will not be hurt by the second death." & ~Revelation 20:6, 14{NIV}~ states, "Blessed and holy is the one who has a part in the first resurrection; over these the second death has no power, but they will be priests of God and of Christ and will reign with him for a thousand years…and death and Hades were thrown into the lake of fire. This is the second death, the lake of fire." This is in sharp contrast to the popular theory of eternal punishing!!

Three special facts to keep in mind: 1. The place of punishment is on the earth. "If the righteous will be rewarded in the earth, how much more the wicked and the sinner!" ~Proverbs 11:31{NASB}~ As the righteous will be ultimately recompensed in the earth, ~Daniel 7:27{NASB}~ states, "Then the sovereignty, the dominion, and the greatness of all the kingdoms under the whole heaven will be given to the people of the saints of the Highest One; His kingdom will be an everlasting kingdom, and all the dominions will serve and obey Him." Matthew 5:5{NASB} states, "Blessed are the gentle, for they shall inherit the earth." Also 2nd Peter 3:13{NASB} states, "But according to His promise we are looking for new heavens and a new earth, in which righteousness dwells." & Revelation 21:1-2{NASB} states, "And I saw a new heaven and a new earth; for the first heaven and the first earth passed away, and there is no longer any sea. And I saw the holy city,

New Jerusalem, coming down out of heaven from God, made ready as a bride adorned for her husband."

In the same manner will the wicked receive their punishment on this earth, see Revelation 20, see also 2nd Peter 3:1-10 for further study. 2. This earth will pass away and will not come to remembrance, "And I saw a new heaven and a new earth; for the first heaven and the first earth passed away, and ther is no longer any sea." ~Revelation 21:1{NASB}~ By using the Greek word Kainos, meaning fresh, new, John is most likely emphasizing the fact that the new heavens and the new earth will be created from the purified elements of the old. This means then that the new heavens and the new earth are a re-creation, a forming together anew of the existing elements, and not a creation ex nihilo. That being true it is clear that the hell-fire in which the wicked will be punished will come to an end when this earth will pass away, as all the wicked will be turned into ashes. "For behold, the day is coming burning like a furnace; and all the arrogant and every evildoer will be chaff; and the day that is coming will set them ablaze,' says the Lord of hosts, so that it will leave them neither root or branch. But for you who fear My name the sun of righteousness will rise with healing in its wings; and you will go forth and skip about like calves from the stall." ~Malachi 4:1-3{NASB}~

~Matthew 3:12{NASB}~ states, "And His winnowing fork is in His hand, and He will thoroughly clear His threshing floor; and He will gather His wheat into the barn but He will burn up the chaff with unquenchable fire." The winnowing fork or shovel was what the ancients used to lift grain from the threshing floor and was thrown against the wind, to separate it from its chaff, see Ruth 3:2. The grain would then fall back to the floor, and the chaff being carried away by the wind to one side, then the chaff would be burned thoroughly, completely. The illustration is that of a farmer beginning at one side of his threshing floor and proceeding systematically across it to the other side. As this scenario plays out, we glimpse a picture of total destruction, as the chaff are burned to ashes by an unquenchable fire. They will be burned so completely that there not be left a root or branch. This scenario lends no credence to the picture of an everlasting fire in which the wicked are tortured endlessly. Scripture emphasizes that the wicked will be burned up so completely, that there will be nothing left of them.

God will make a new heaven and a new earth, which will be the home of the redeemed for ever and ever. "For behold, I create new heavens and a new earth; and the former things shall not be remembered or come to mind." ~Isaiah 65:17{NASB}~ ~Isaiah 66:22-23{NASB}~ states, "For just as the new heavens and the new earth which I make will endure before Me,' declares the Lord, 'So your offspring and your name will endure. And it shall be from new moon to new moon and from sabbath to sabbath, all mankind will come to bow down before Me,' says the Lord." The seventh day Sabbath is an eternal institution, and will be honored by the saints in the new earth to come. All will observe the seventh day Sabbath in recognition of the eternal creator of the world, who is Jesus Christ Himself. They will also keep the seventh day Sabbath in the Edenic bliss as a memorial of the re-Creator of the new heavens and the new earth of righteousness and holiness.

Summary: 1. God's strange act will be when He will have to destroy men that He made to live to His glory. 2. He will do this act in spite of His effort to keep from doing it. 3. When men will suffer eternal hell-fire, it will be their own fault; they, and not God, choose to suffer the punishment intended for the devil and his angels. 4. How wonderful it is to know that none of us need to suffer punishment in hell. 5. Why choose death and not life. 6. God help us to find the soul-saving answer to this question.

THE MODERN JEW IN BIBLE PROPHECY

By Pastor Fred L. Grant

The modern Jew in the light of Bible prophecy. First the modern state of Israel has been a problem child for the United Nations, and the Arab League seeks to destroy the state of Israel. There are some theologians who claim that the state of Israel is the answer to Bible prophecy, that the prophets foretold the reconstituting of Israel as a state shortly prior to the second coming of Christ. In this light, let's take a brief look at the modern Jew in the light of Bible prophecy.

The origin and meaning of the name Israel. It was given by the angel of the Lord, to Jacob, at the ford of Jabbok. ~Genesis 32:22-28{NASB}~ states, "Now he arose that same night and took his two wives and his two maids and his eleven children, and crossed the ford of the Jabbok. He took them and sent them across the stream. And he sent across whatever he had. Jacob Wrestles. Then Jacob was left alone, and a man wrestled with him until daybreak. When he saw that he had not prevailed against him, he touched the socket of his thigh; so the socket of Jacob's thigh was dislocated while he wrestled with him. Then he said, 'Let me go, for the dawn is breaking.' But he said, 'I will not let you go unless you bless me.' So he said to him, 'What is your name?' And he said, "Jacob." He said, "Your name shall no longer be Jacob, but Israel; for you have striven with God and with men and have prevailed.'" Verse 28 of Genesis 32 signifies a prince having power with God and man prevailing.

An Israelite is one in whom there is found no guile. ~John 1:47{NASB}~ states, "Jesus saw Nathanael coming to Him, and said of him, 'Behold, an Israelite indeed, in whom is no guile!'" also ~Zephaniah 3:13{NASB}~ states, "The remnant of Israel will do no wrong and tell no lies, nor will a deceitful tongue be found in their mouths; for they shall feed and lied down with no one to make them tremble." Any person circumcised in the heart is a true Israelite, as ~Romans 2:28-29{NASB}~ states, "For he is not a Jew who is one outwardly; neither is circumcision that which is outward in the flesh. But he is a Jew who is one inwardly; and circumcision is that which is of the heart, by the Spirit, not by the letter; and his praise is not from men, but from God." Any and all who are Christ's are Israelites. ~Galatians 3:26-29{NASB}~ states, "For you are all sons of God through faith in Christ Jesus. For all of you who were baptized into Christ have clothed yourselves with Christ. There is neither Jew nor Greek, there is neither slave nor free man, there is neither male nor female; for you are all one in Christ Jesus. And if you belong to Christ, then you are Abraham's descendants, heirs according to promise."

This shows that the name 'Israel' is of spiritual origin and is a misnomer when applied to the flesh. ~Romans 9:6-8{NASB}~ states, "But it is not as though the word of God has failed. For they are not all Israel who are descended from Israel; nor are they all children because they are Abraham's descendants, but: through Isaac your descendants will be named. That is, it is not the children of the flesh who are children of God, but the children of the promise are regarded as descendants." There are two kinds of Israel. First: Israel after the flesh, ~1st Corinthians 10:18{NASB}~ which states, "Look at the nation Israel; are not those who eat the sacrifices sharers in the altar?" They are symbolized by Ishmael, son of the bond woman Hagar, ~Galatians 4:21-28{NASB}~ "Bond and Free. Tell me, you who want to be under law, do you not listen to the law? For it is written that Abraham had two sons, one by the bondwoman and one by the free woman. But the son by the bondwoman was born according to the flesh, and the son by the free woman through the promise. This is allegorically speaking, for these women are two covenants: one proceeding from Mount Sinai bearing children who are to be slaves; she is Hagar. Now this Hagar is Mount Sinai in Arabia and corresponds to the present Jerusalem, for she is in slavery with her children. But the Jerusalem above is free; she is our mother. For it is written, "Rejoice, barren woman who does not bear;

Break forth and shout, you who are not in labor; for more numerous are the children of the desolate than of the one who has a husband." And you brethren, like Isaac, are children of promise." They are a false seed, ~Isaiah 57:4, 11{NASB}~ states, "Against whom do you jest? Against whom do you open wide your mouth and stick out your tongue? Are you not children of rebellion, offspring of deceit…Of whom were you worried and fearful, when you lied, and did not remember Me, nor give Me a thought? Was I not silent even for a long time so you do not fear Me?"

Second: Israel of God. ~Galatians 6:16{NASB}~ states, "And those who will walk by this rule, peace and mercy be upon them, and upon the Israel of God." This is symbolized by Isaac, the son of the free woman. ~Galatians 4:31{NASB}~ states, "So then, brethren, we are not children of a bondwoman, but of the free woman." This is the seed of the promise made to Abraham, ~Romans 9:6-9{NASB}~ states, "But it is not as though the word of God has failed. For they are not all Israel who are descended from Israel; neither are they all children because they are Abraham's descendants, but: through Isaac your descendants will be named. That is, it is not the children of the flesh who are children of God, but the children of the promise are regarded as descendants. For this is a word of promise: At this time I will come, and Sarah shall have a son."

Consider prayerfully with me God's promises to Abraham and his seed. The seed of Abraham, to whom God made the promise, is none other than Jesus Christ our Lord and savior. ~Galatians 3:16{NASB}~ states, "Now the promises were spoken to Abraham and to his seed. He does not say, 'And to his seeds.' As referring to many, but rather to one, 'And to your seed,' that is Christ." Christ and Christ alone is the true heir to God's eternal promise. ~Hebrews 3:1-3{NASB}~ states, "Therefore, holy brethren, partakers of a heavenly calling, consider Jesus, the Apostle and High Priest of our confession; He was faithful to Him who appointed Him, as Moses also was in all His house. For He has been counted worthy of more glory than Moses, by just so much as the builder of the house has more honor than the house." The Jews knew that, ~Matthew 21:37-38(NASB}~ states, "But afterward he sent his son to them, saying, 'They will respect my son.' But when the vine-growers saw the son, they said among themselves, 'This is the heir; come, let us kill him, and seize his inheritance."

All who accept Jesus Christ as their personal savior become fellow heirs with Christ to all God's promises. ~Galatians 3:26-29{NASB}~ "For you are all sons of God through faith in Christ Jesus. For all of you who were baptized into Christ have clothed yourselves with Christ. There is neither Jew nor Greek, there is neither slave nor free man, there is neither male nor female; for you are all one in Christ Jesus. And if you belong to Christ, then you are Abraham's descendants, heirs according to promise." ~Romans 8:17{NASB}~ states, "And if children, heirs also, heirs of God and fellow heirs with Christ, if indeed we suffer with Him in order that we may also be glorified with Him."

It is imperative to remember that God is no respecter of persons. ~Acts 10:34-35{NASB}~ states, " And opening his mouth, Peter said: 'I most certainly understand now that God is not one to show partiality, but in every nation the man who fears Him and does what is right is welcome to Him." ~Job 34:19{NASB}~ states, "Who shows no partiality to princes, nor regards the rich above the poor, for they all are the work of His hands." Also ~Romans 2:11{NASB}~ states, "For there is no partiality with God." The new birth is the key to sonship in Christ. ~John 3:3-9{NASB}~ Jesus answered and said to him, 'Truly, truly, I say to you, unless one is born again he cannot see the kingdom of God.' 'Nicodemus said to Him, 'How can a man be born when he is old? He cannot enter a second time into his mother's womb and be born, can he?' Jesus answered, 'Truly, truly, I say to you, unless one is born of water and the Spirit he cannot enter into the kingdom of God. That which is born of the flesh is flesh, and that which is born of the Spirit is spirit. Do not be amazed that I said to you, 'You must be born again.' The wind blows where it wishes and you hear the sound of it, but do not know where it comes from and where it is going; so is everyone who is born of the Spirit.' Nicodemus said to Him, 'How can these things be?'" ~Romans 8:14-17{NASB}~ states, "For all who are being led by the Spirit of God, these are sons of God. For you have not received a spirit of slavery leading to fear again, but you have received a spirit of adoption as sons by which we cry out, "Abba! Father!" The Spirit Himself testifies with our spirit that we are children of God, and if children, heirs also, heirs of God and fellow heirs with Christ, if indeed we suffer with Him so that we may also be glorified with Him."

Flesh and blood are excluded. ~John 1:12-13{NASB}~ states, "But as many as received Him, to them He gave the right to become children of God, even to those who believe in His name, who were born not of blood, nor of the will of the flesh, nor of the will of man, but of God." ~1st Corinthians 15:50{NASB}~ states, "Now I say this, brethren, that flesh and blood cannot inherit the kingdom of God; nor does the perishable inherit the imperishable." Character and not blood relation, is what qualifies anyone to be an heir to God's promises. Character comes to us when we become partakers of the divine nature. ~Ephesians 3:6{NASB}~ states, "To be specific, that the Gentiles are fellow heirs and fellow members of the body, and fellow partakers of the promise in Christ Jesus through the gospel." ~2nd Peter 1:2-9{NASB}~ states, "Grace and peace be multiplied to you in the knowledge of God and of Jesus our Lord; seeing that His divine power has granted to us everything pertaining to life and godliness, through the true knowledge of Him who called us by His own glory and excellence. For by these He has granted to us His precious and magnificent promises, so that by them you may become partakers of the divine nature, having escaped the corruption that is in the world by lust. Now for this very reason also, applying all diligence, in your faith supply moral excellence, and in your moral excellence, knowledge, and in your knowledge, self-control, and in your self-control, perseverance, and in your perseverance, godliness, and in your godliness, brotherly kindness, and in your brotherly kindness, love. For if these qualities are yours and are increasing, they render you neither useless nor unfruitful in the true knowledge of our Lord Jesus Christ. For he who lacks these qualities is blind or short-sighted, having forgotten his purification from his former sins."

One of the missions of Christ was to remove the wall of partition, set up by the selfishness of sinful human beings. ~Ephesians 2:11-16{NASB}~ states, "Therefore remember that formerly you, the Gentiles in the flesh, who are called 'Uncircumcision' by the so-called 'Circumcision,' which is performed in the flesh by human hands—remember that you were at that time separate from Christ, excluded from the commonwealth of Israel, and strangers to the covenants of promise, having no hope and without God in the world. But now in Christ Jesus you who formerly were far off have been brought near by the blood of Christ. For He Himself is our peace, who made both groups into one and broke down the barrier of the dividing wall, by abolishing in His flesh the enmity, which is the Law of commandments contained in ordinances, so that in Himself He might make the two into one new man, thus establishing peace, and might reconcile them both in one body to God through the cross, by it having put to death the enmity." Christ did this to bring into union all men into one faith and one hope through the preaching of the gospel of Jesus Christ. Compare Ephesians 2:11-16 with ~Ephesians 1:10-12{NASB}~ which states, "With a view to an administration suitable to the fullness of the times, that is, the summing up of things in Christ, things in the heavens and things upon the earth, also we have obtained an inheritance, having been predestined according to His purpose who works all things after the council of His will, to the end that we who were the first to hope in Christ should be to the praise of His glory."

Christ considered this objective a must. ~John 10:15-16{NASB}~ states, "Even as the Father knows Me and I know the Father; and I lay down My life for the sheep. And I have other sheep, which are not of this fold; I must bring them also, and they shall hear My voice; and they shall become one flock with one shepherd." The modern Jew occupies the same place in the scheme of God as does any other sinner for whom Christ died. ~Galatians 3:26-29{NASB}~ states, "For you are all sons of God through faith in Christ Jesus. For all of you who were baptized into Christ have clothed yourselves with Christ. There is neither Jew nor Greek, there is neither slave nor free man, there is neither male nor female; for you are all one in Christ Jesus. And if you belong to Christ, then you are Abraham's descendants, heirs according to promise."